HARMONIZE YOUR LIFE

HARMONIZE YOUR LIFE

FINDING ALIGNMENT FROM WITHIN

DR. SAM MARCH

SB PRESS

Harmonize Your Life: Finding Alignment From Within

Published by StoryBuilders Press.

978-1-954521-87-2 - eBook
978-1-954521-88-9 - Paperback
978-1-954521-89-6 - Hardcover

This book is dedicated to my boys—Jon and Jordan.
You are my muse and inspired harmony.

CONTENTS

Chapter 1

YOU'RE NOT BROKEN

I thought surviving was normal, but I had no idea what living really felt like.

Growing up, headaches were just part of life. I thought everybody had them. I remember waking up in the morning with that dull throb behind my eyes, and by 2 p.m. in the afternoon, it would turn into this pounding that made it hard to even think straight. But, you know, as a kid, I just dealt with it. I figured, *"This is normal, right? Everyone gets headaches."*

So I didn't complain, I didn't say much—I just pushed through the daily pain. As I always say: "It is what it is."

I thought surviving was normal, but I had no idea what living really felt like.

Well, until it's not. After a while, I started to see a glare. That was enough for my parents to finally take me to a doctor. I remember waiting for the eye doctor in her office, thinking, *"Finally, maybe this will help with these headaches."* The glare from the light was unbearable, like it was attacking my eyes every day.

As I sat hopeful in the optometrist chair, expecting some kind of solution, the doctor looked at me and said, "You have 20/20 vision."

Confused at her dismissal, I tentatively asked, "Okay . . . so why am I still in pain?" In response, she handed me a pair of large glasses

1

to help with the glare. Obediently, I put them on with what little hope I had left, thinking maybe this will finally fix things.

Spoiler alert: it didn't.

The headaches didn't go away. In fact, I had to figure out how to wear the glasses in a way that wouldn't make the glare worse. Can you imagine? I had to move my head a certain way just to avoid the light coming through. It was ridiculous, and yet, I wore them everywhere—outside, even inside—these large polarized glasses that made me stick out like a sore thumb.

These glasses were a cruel joke that I worried my friends wouldn't get. Were they judging me? Or wondering, "Why is Samantha wearing those strange glasses all the time?" It made me feel so out of place; it wasn't just frustrating—it was lonely. The glasses didn't help, the doctors didn't help, and my headaches were still there.

It felt like my body was fighting me, and I had no idea why.

The chronic headache pain never went away. Instead, it began to seep into more areas of my life. As a teenager, I thought I was just unlucky when it came to my periods. Every month, it was the same thing—cramps so bad I couldn't even stand up straight, let alone go to school or hang out with my friends. I'd lie on my bed, curled up, trying not to cry, thinking, *"This is just what girls deal with, right?"* I didn't know any better. I remember taking all kinds of painkillers, but they didn't do a thing. It felt like my body was fighting me, and I had no idea why.

My entire childhood was marked with visits to different doctors, taking suggested medications, but walking away with the same pain. Nothing helped because "nothing was wrong." And what did a young girl like me know compared to these qualified doctors with medical degrees? I forced myself to think, *"This is normal. People deal with this kind of pain all the time. I'm strong enough to push through. I'm fine."*

As I grew up and began to plan for my future, one thing was certain: I hated medication—didn't trust it, didn't like it, and definitely didn't want it in my body. But deep down, I always had this desire to help people, and I knew there had to be a better way to do it. At first, I thought I'd become a doctor, you know, the traditional kind. But as I got deeper into my studies, something didn't sit right with me. I didn't want to be that doctor just handing out prescriptions, but what else was there?

At nineteen, everything changed. I remember sitting in church one day, just minding my own business, when a chiropractor showed up to give a health talk. Now, I wasn't even paying full attention to him at first—I mean, I had lived with headaches, back pain, and everything else for years at that point. I thought it was just normal.

But then he said something that hit me: "Your spine controls everything."

Wait, what . . .?

Suddenly, I was paying very close attention to everything this doctor was saying about spinal misalignment affecting your whole body. *"Hold up, maybe this is why I feel like my body's falling apart."*

After the talk, I was beyond curious. I signed up for his $40 introductory chiropractic special, because listen, I was a broke college student and $40 was all I could swing. I walked into his office for the first time, filled out the forms, didn't even mention the headaches or the daily back pain. Because . . . why would I? Nothing was wrong with me. Those symptoms had nothing to do with my spine, right? I just wanted to see what my spine looked like. He took X-rays, and a few days later, I came back for the results.

Now, let me tell you, when I walked into that room and saw my X-rays, my jaw hit the floor. *"This cannot be me. No way."* I immediately walked out to the front desk and said, "I think there's been a mistake. Those are not my X-rays." Rightfully, the staff freaked out because of HIPAA, and they rushed in to check the X-rays on the screen.

Nope, they're mine.

The doctor came in and pointed at the screen, and I'll never forget the image—my neck was completely forward. He simply stated, "You have double scoliosis. You're in phase two degeneration, and you're only nineteen years old." My brain couldn't process it. I had no idea what phase two even meant, but I knew it wasn't good.

Next, he looked at my intake form. He was shocked that none of the symptom boxes had been checked. He asked, "I see that you didn't mention any symptoms, are you sure?" When I replied no, because "nothing was wrong," he started listing off possible symptoms based on where my misalignments were located: headaches, trouble sleeping, anxiety, even depression. In my mind, I was saying, *"Check, check, check . . ."*

It was like I had been given my life back, piece by piece, with each adjustment.

I couldn't believe it; I had been living with all of this for years, thinking it was just *normal*. He talked about my lower back and how it's connected to the excruciating menstrual pain I had had for as long as I could remember. Everything he said was like a lightbulb going off in my head, piece by piece.

The real kicker? He asked me if I wanted to fix it. I thought, *"Of course I want to fix it, but is this even possible? Can my body really change after all these years of pain?"* And that's when he told me it was. I was sold; I paid for my own treatment with student loan money—didn't ask anyone for help—and that was it.

For the first time in over seven years, I started to live without pain. No daily headaches, no constant back pain, not being chained to migraines. It was like I had been given my life back, piece by piece, with each adjustment.

That's when I realized—I hadn't been living; I'd been surviving. And this was the moment that changed everything.

Working with a Chiropractor Changed My Life

I'm Dr. Sam March, and I was that nineteen-year-old girl. I was so used to surviving that I didn't even know what living felt like anymore. So when Dr. David Yachter, the chiropractor that presented at my church, took one look at my X-rays and told me how out of alignment I was—both physically and in life—it got my attention. None of the missed diagnoses over my life mattered anymore—because he told me everything I needed to hear.

That day, *I learned that my body wasn't broken*—it was just trying to tell me something, and I'd finally found someone who could help me listen. My body had the blueprint for healing all along; it just needed the right push. Six weeks. That's how long it took before I started noticing real changes. The migraines that had ruled my life? Gone. The cramps that used to knock me out? Gone.

After months of working with him, I woke up one day and realized: I was *free* from pain for the first time in years. I wasn't broken; I had just been living in survival mode. But now, I was living—really living. My digestion improved, I was thinking clearer, sleeping better, and that double scoliosis that could've kept me from having my kids? It was *corrected*. If I hadn't gone through this, I wouldn't have my two beautiful children today, and I can't imagine my life without them.

What I learned in that moment is something I carry with me every day: pain is an alarm system, not a measure of health. By the time you feel it, the problem has been there for a while. That realization changed my life, and it's why I became a chiropractor. My mission is to help other women understand that

Pain is an alarm system, not a measure of health.

you don't have to live in pain, and you don't have to settle for surviving when you can thrive. Harmony is the goal—not perfection, because life isn't about having everything perfectly in place.

You've probably gotten so used to the limits that you can't even imagine living without them.

I went from a life where I expected pain every day, to one filled with possibilities. Feeling better opened doors I didn't even know were closed. My mental health shifted, my world expanded, and suddenly, the things I used to tell myself I couldn't do—travel, try new activities, even connect more with others—they became realities. And listen, if you're anything like I was at nineteen, it's hard to believe that life can be different. You've probably gotten so used to the limits that you can't even imagine living without them.

Maybe you're a new mom, feeling like you're stuck on the back burner while everyone else focuses on the baby. Or maybe you're grinding at work, and by the time you get home, the last thing you want to think about is taking care of *yourself.* Or you've convinced yourself that the pain and fatigue you feel every day are just part of the deal. That's where I was—thinking that surviving was normal.

All of that to say, it's *not* normal. And you are *not* broken. You are worthy of a life that doesn't revolve around pain. You deserve to feel good. And I know it's going to take time, energy, maybe even some money, but I promise you—it's

You are worthy of a life that doesn't revolve around pain.

worth it. You've already taken the first step by picking up this book, and that's huge. Your body, mind, and spirit are capable of healing, but it's going to take work. And when you get to the other side, the person you were before? She'll feel like a distant memory, someone you barely recognize. And that's when you'll know—you've truly stepped into your life.

Harmony, Not Perfection, is the Goal

I've always believed that harmony in life isn't about perfection—it's about finding alignment, even in the chaos. I learned that firsthand. Growing up, my dad kept the radio on *all the time.* It didn't matter if he was home or away for days, that music was always playing. Gospel, jazz, reggae, you name it. There was no quiet, just this constant stream of sound that filled our home. And in a way, that radio taught me something—I realized life is like that radio, always playing, even when we're not paying attention. Sometimes, the music is smooth and easy, and other times it's loud and chaotic, but it's always there, creating a rhythm we need to find our harmony in.

That's what I had to do when my life hit the hard notes. Going through a separation and divorce while raising my children wasn't just emotionally draining—it forced me to take a hard look at how I was showing up in my life. I wasn't just reacting to my circumstances; I was *living* in survival mode, thinking that was normal. But deep down, I knew something was out of alignment. I had to go deeper and do the hard work of figuring out why I made the choices I did, why I felt the way I did, and how I could heal.

And just like that radio always playing, our bodies and minds are always talking to us, always giving us signals. The problem is, we often ignore them. In my work as a chiropractor, I've seen how past and present trauma—whether it's emotional or physical—shows up in the body. Stress changes your posture, tightens your muscles, shifts your alignment. You might walk down the hall at work with your shoulders slouched, feeling like the weight of the world is on you, and over time, that stress turns into neck pain, back pain, migraines. And yeah, you can come to me for an adjustment, but if you don't deal with the *root cause*, those same physical problems will keep coming back.

That's when I realized my purpose wasn't just to fix bodies—it was to help people connect the dots between their mind, their emotions, and their physical health. Because listen, wellness isn't just about how much you exercise or what you eat. It's about living in alignment—mentally, emotionally, spiritually. That's where real healing happens. You have to understand how everything bobs and weaves together, like instruments in a song. If one part is out of tune, the whole thing feels off.

When I went on a mindfulness retreat a few years back, I got a chance to hit pause and listen to the rhythm of my own life. I dug deep into my triggers, my pain, my emotions, and found out where they were really coming from. It wasn't pretty, but it was necessary. That retreat was the beginning of a new lifetime journey. It

> *Healing is about more than just treating symptoms— it's about finding harmony within yourself.*

gave me the tools to enable response instead of reaction. I understood myself better, and it made me realize that healing is about more than just treating symptoms—it's about finding harmony within yourself, just like my dad's radio playing every day without fail.

Living in alignment takes work, and it starts with being honest with yourself.

If you're here with me, reading this book, it's because something feels out of alignment in your life. Maybe you're tired of walking through life feeling like something's missing, like you're always a step behind your own needs. Trust me, I've been there. But living in alignment takes work, and it starts with being honest with yourself. You have to listen to the signals your body and mind are sending you, and choose to make the conscious decisions that will lead to healing.

This isn't just about adjusting your posture—it's about adjusting your mindset, your emotions, and your spirit. This is your chance to start living. And trust me, you are worth every bit of effort it takes to get there.

Rmoniz ™ Method: The 6 Cs of Harmony

Let me tell you, there's a big difference between chasing balance and embracing *harmony* in your life. Balance? It trips people up because it makes us think everything has to be perfectly even, like you're supposed to have it all together all the time. Guess what? That's not realistic. Maybe one leg's a little longer than the other, maybe your daily routine is all over the place, and maybe you've never had a "balanced" day in your life. And you know what? That's okay! Balance makes it easy to feel like you're falling short, like you're not measuring up. But harmony? That's where the magic is.

Harmony is about flow, not perfection. Life has its ups and downs, its fast and slow moments, and sometimes it's downright chaotic. But here's the thing: your job isn't to keep everything perfectly balanced—it's to keep playing. It's time to stop fighting for some kind of rigid equality in your life and instead *find the beauty* in the unique rhythm that's yours. Some days, your notes are going to be high and light; other days, they'll be heavy and low. But it's all part of your soundtrack. Let's figure out the chords that feel right for you, and help you start playing them in a way that brings you joy, not stress.

Let me tell you, there's a big difference between chasing balance and embracing harmony in your life.

My goal? To help you find that inner sense of *harmony*, where your mind, body, and spirit are in sync with what feels right for you. No more forcing things to fit into a "balanced" box—let's work with the flow of your life and create something beautiful from it.

Awareness is the first step. You can't fix what you don't see, right? That's where we start. I'm going to help you bring those hidden thoughts, feelings, and behaviors up to the surface so you can understand why they're there and how to work through them. Together, we'll dig into the triggers, traumas, and toxins that have thrown off your alignment over the years, and we'll learn how to embrace the chaos and turn it into something that works for you. It's about finding your alignment—not just in your spine, but in your whole life.

Throughout this journey, you'll learn how to Rmoniz™ and use my 6 Cs of Harmony—practical actions you can take to start healing from the inside out, because real harmony comes from within. So let's get started and help you rediscover who you really are, and live in a way that lets you live in alignment, fully and unapologetically. Here's a preview of the journey you'll take with the 6 Cs.

Cultivate a Growth Mindset

Mindset is everything. We all have one—it's the lens through which we see the world—but most of us aren't using it to its full potential. The best part? You have the power to change it. Yeah, *you* have that power.

> *The minute you choose to shift your mindset, the whole game changes.*

When your mindset leans negative, it's like wearing the wrong prescription glasses. Everything gets distorted. You start talking down to yourself, feeling unworthy, and convinced that life is about surviving, not thriving. It shrinks your world. You find yourself thinking small, living small, and believing that's all you deserve.

But here's the good news: *the minute you choose to shift your mindset, the whole game changes.* You start becoming your own best friend instead of your harshest critic. Your self-talk? It gets kinder. You start seeing opportunities where you once saw obstacles, and suddenly, those self-imposed limits? Gone. You realize just how much power you've had all along, and the possibilities start expanding in ways you never imagined.

In Chapter Four, we're going to dig deep into what makes a healthy mindset versus an unhealthy one. You'll learn how to *respond* instead of react. That's where freedom is—breaking out of that victim mentality that keeps you stuck. It's time to step into your power, shift your mindset, and live life in a way that feels *full* of possibilities.

Connect with Your Emotions

Here's the real deal: when you ignore your emotions, they don't just disappear—they stick around, and over time, they show up in your body as physical issues. Yep, that tension in your shoulders, the headaches, that constant tightness you feel—it's your body holding on to all those emotions you've been pushing aside. When my team and I work with clients, our main goal is to help them find *harmony* in their bodies. And to do that, we've got to get real about their emotions. The only way to harmonize your energy is to connect with it, to understand it.

Think about it this way: we all have chaos in our lives. No one's exempt from it. But here's the thing—running from that chaos or pretending it's not there doesn't work. You've got to *connect* to it. Your emotions are feedback. They're not something to shove aside; they're there to guide you. I know, I know—sometimes it

Your emotions are feedback. They're not something to shove aside; they're there to guide you.

feels easier to just push those feelings down, keep it moving, and not deal with them. But let me tell you, ignored emotions don't go away. They become *stored* emotions. And when you don't deal with them, trust me, they'll find a way to deal with *you*. One tiny trigger, and suddenly you're exploding, wondering, *"Where did that even come from?"*

In Chapter Five, we're diving deep into this. You'll learn why it's so important to come face-to-face with your emotions. I'll walk you through my favorite strategies to help you address, process, and finally release those unprocessed feelings. It's time to stop letting them hold you back and start using them as a path to better health and *real* harmony.

Care for Your Physical Well-Being

Alright, I know what you're thinking—this isn't news. We *all* know we need to exercise. But let's be real—*knowing* it and actually *doing* it are two totally different things. Prioritizing your physical health can feel like a struggle when life gets busy. But here's the kicker: motion literally brings nutrition to your brain, and your brain helps to control your emotions. It's all connected. Ever notice how when you're feeling low, you barely want to move? But when you're excited, you can't sit still? That's not just a coincidence. Your emotions are tied to your body's movement, and when you get stuck in one, the other follows.

In Chapter Six, we're going way beyond the usual "you should exercise" talk. I'm going to show you how stretching and flexibility in your body can actually make you more flexible in your life. Yep, you heard that right—physical flexibility spills over into your mindset and emotional health. You'll get my favorite tips on how to create a consistent routine that fits into your life, so you can experience the benefits of mobility firsthand. Trust me, once you start moving, you'll be amazed at how it shifts everything.

Channel Positive Energy

When I decided to own how I was feeling and really started putting in the work on myself, it was like getting an instrument in tune—I fell into harmony with my life. I'll never forget running into a friend who looked at me and said, "I don't know what you're doing, but whatever it is, *keep doing it*—you're glowing!" And she was right. She could see it before I even fully realized it myself. My spirit was shining through in a way it never had before, and hearing that from her was the confirmation I didn't know I needed.

The more you take care of your physical and emotional needs, the more room you make for positivity in your life. When you decide to *really* prioritize yourself, that inner harmony shines through for everyone to see. It's like you're finally stepping into the version of yourself you were always meant to be.

In Chapter Seven, we're going to dig into how to notice when your spirit's feeling low and, more importantly, how to bring that energy back up. I'll share some of my favorite ways to raise your vibe and get your harmony in tune. It's time to let the world see the real you—because trust me, when you're glowing, people notice!

The more you take care of your physical and emotional needs, the more room you make for positivity in your life.

Celebrate Life's Abundance

Everyone is *worthy* of abundance. But when you've been living with things out of tune, it's easy to keep searching for the next note out of tune, waiting for the next bad thing to happen, instead of getting aligned with the music that's all around you. Do you know what I'm saying?

Look, I get it. It's normal to feel like, "Okay, things are going well, but when's the other shoe going to drop?" But here's the truth: you don't have to live like that anymore. You don't have to keep living in fear, thinking you're not worthy of a beautiful, abundant life.

You don't have to keep living in fear, thinking you're not worthy of a beautiful, abundant life.

When you start experiencing more good than bad, it's crucial to recognize that those old negative stories are just that—*stories*. They don't define you. You are worthy of all the incredible opportunities and blessings coming your way. It's time to stop questioning if you deserve them and start believing that you *do*.

In Chapter Eight, we're going to work on strengthening that self-awareness so you can catch yourself when you're treating the good things in your life as if they're just temporary. I'll show you how to greet abundance with open arms and love, instead of fear and doubt. You'll learn tools to remind yourself that you are *more than worthy* of all the prosperity and harmony that comes your way. Let's turn that life radio all the way up.

Create Meaningful Connections

We're all connected in this life. As human beings, we were made to be social, to lean on each other, and to grow together. But so many of us feel like we've got to suffer in silence, like we can only reach out when everything in our life is aligned and harmonizing. Let me tell you, *that's not how it works.* Your harmony is going to ebb and flow—it's just part of the journey.

You're *not* alone in this, whether you're completely in harmony or horribly off tune. What matters is that you keep moving forward. The more you connect with others, the easier it becomes to live in alignment. There's so much strength in community, and when you surround yourself with people who are on a growth path like you, that harmony gets even sweeter.

In Chapter Nine, I'm excited to share ways you can connect with chiropractors in person and how to build a strong support system both online and offline with people who are just as committed to their growth as you are. Because trust me, we're in this together, and life is always better when you've got a community walking with you on the journey.

Once you finish this book, you're not going to magically feel 100% healed and perfectly aligned. Life doesn't work that way, and neither does healing. Just like when you get a chiropractic adjustment, your body has to get used to that new alignment. There's going to be some tension as you learn to live in harmony with *all* parts of yourself—physically, emotionally, and spiritually. Picture it like tuning an instrument. At first, the strings might feel tight, maybe even out of tune, but as you keep working on it, everything starts to flow together. The notes become clear, and suddenly, you've got *harmony.* That's how it works when you commit to this process.

The key? You'll be *empowered*. You'll have the tools and the awareness to make choices that lead to less pain and more peace. And just like a well-tuned instrument, when things fall into place, your body, mind, and spirit can play together in a way that feels aligned—even if life gets chaotic around you.

Look, my life didn't get less stressful just because I started doing the healing work—I still had stress because that's real life. But here's the thing: I don't *feel* the stress in my body like I used to. I feel lighter, more at ease. I have the tools to take care of myself, to process my emotions, and to relax, even when life decides to throw a curveball.

All of that to say, the real gift of this journey is that you'll know how to handle it in a way that doesn't break you down. You don't need to hide the messy, off-key parts of yourself anymore. By strengthening your self-awareness, you'll be able to step back and observe those negative feelings, kind of like catching an out-of-tune note, and instead of being swept away by them, you'll learn to adjust. Facing that disharmony is *brave*, and it's the only way to see that you already have what it takes to handle whatever life throws your way.

Time to Reflect

As we keep moving together on this journey, I'm going to offer you some practical ways to really lock in what you're learning. There might be action steps, or I might throw a few questions your way to help strengthen that self-awareness muscle. Right now, I just want you to take a step back and reflect. When I work face-to-face with my clients, one of the first things I help them do is understand *why* they want to make changes. Because by knowing what you're working toward, that's the fuel that keeps you going, especially when life throws its highs and lows your way.

If journaling is your thing, go ahead and grab that notebook. Write it out, get real with yourself, and let the words flow. This is your chance to check in with *you* and really understand what's driving your journey. Let's start there, because once you've got that clarity, everything else gets a little easier.

If you had no pain, how would that change your life?

What would you be able to do that you aren't able to do now?

Why is it important for you to be able to do those things?

How would being able to do those things elevate your happiness and joy?

Chapter 2

STAYING IN TUNE

When I got off that adjustment table for the first time, I remember I took a breath—a deep, full, uninterrupted breath. The sharp, constant ache in my mid-back I'd grown used to was suddenly gone, like a veil had been lifted. I remember thinking, *"This can't be real; pain doesn't just disappear."* But there I was, standing there, feeling lighter, even freer. It wasn't just the absence of pain—it was like my body was waking up, like parts of me I didn't even know had been numb were finally alive again. And for the first time in years, I could just exist without feeling weighed down by an invisible anchor.

That night, I slept better than I had in months. Usually, I'd toss and turn, trying to get comfortable, the pain keeping me half-awake through every hour. But this time, my body relaxed, and I drifted into the deepest, most peaceful sleep. Waking up that next morning, I felt rejuvenated. I wasn't just rested; I felt restored, like something foundational in me had shifted back into place. I even looked at myself in the mirror a little differently, noticing a hint of energy in my eyes I hadn't seen in years.

In the days that followed, I started realizing just how much my pain had limited me. I joined the walking club at my church, something I'd avoided because I'd always end up with a migraine from the glare of being outside if I tried. So, there I was—with the walking club at my church, ready to tackle a mile and a half in the South Florida heat. Now, this was a group full of power-walkers,

17

speed-walkers, and casual strollers, but that sunshine and heat didn't play. Usually, I would've skipped, knowing I'd be hit with a migraine by the time we finished. But after my first adjustment, I thought, *"Let's see what this body can do now."*

So, I laced up, grabbed my sunglasses, and joined in. And let me tell you, that morning, I wasn't just walking—I was speed-walking. I was moving so fast that even the joggers couldn't keep up! They kept looking over at me like, "Girl, slow down!" I laughed and thought, *"Catch me if you can!"* It was the first time in a long time that I felt like I had this boundless energy flowing through me.

Afterward, we'd all gather for breakfast, a simple spread of fruits, veggies, and the best vegan treats from our church community. As I sat there, talking and laughing, I realized something. I wasn't distracted by pain. I wasn't holding back, thinking about the inevitable headache that was bound to hit at 2 p.m.

> *I realized health wasn't just about pain going away—it was about feeling vibrant, about living fully in each moment.*

Instead, I was present, genuinely there with my friends, building connections that would last, friendships that would walk with me through the years. That walking club didn't just get me moving; it gave me back a piece of myself. I realized health wasn't just about pain going away—it was about feeling vibrant, about living fully in each moment. And as I looked around at my church family, eating and laughing under the trees, I thought, *"This—this is what healing really feels like."*

After that initial year of adjustments, I was feeling amazing—clear mind, high energy, breathing deep and easy. So, naturally, I ended my routine of adjustments (remember, I was on a college student budget!) and I told myself, *"I'm good; I don't need to keep this up anymore."* And I embarked on a new adventure: a trip overseas for four months across ten countries. I was healthy, I felt in alignment, and my body was in harmony.

But as the trip went on, I started noticing subtle shifts. It wasn't immediate, but little by little, my body wasn't feeling as tuned as it used to. There was a tension creeping back in, a tightness, even some sharp pain with every deep breath. I could tell that the harmony I'd found was starting to slip.

By the time I returned, I was in rough shape. I remember going back to my chiropractor, almost embarrassed that I'd waited so long. It had been a year and a half since my last adjustment, and I could feel the difference. When he took X-rays, it was clear—the curve in my spine had increased again. It wasn't back to the scoliosis stage, thank God, but it was a stark reminder that this wasn't a one-and-done situation. My body needed consistent support to stay aligned, and I couldn't ignore that anymore.

> *Healing isn't about just fixing things once; it's about maintaining harmony, keeping everything tuned like an instrument.*

After that first adjustment coming back, it felt like my body was sighing with relief. That's when it hit me—healing isn't about just fixing things once; it's about maintaining harmony, keeping everything tuned like an instrument. Just because I felt good didn't mean I was done. Health, I realized, isn't something you set and forget. It's something you nurture and fine-tune constantly.

Vertebral Subluxation

Let's put my Dr. Sam hat on for a moment: I want to teach you about vertebral subluxation. It's a medical term that may sound overwhelming or fancy, but let's figure this out together. When you look at the Latin roots of the term "subluxation," "sub" means "below" and "lux" means "light." When there is vertebral subluxation, you are dealing with an area of your spine that is out of alignment. That lack of alignment can keep your light from flowing correctly, affecting how you feel, and ultimately, how you live your life.

Vertebral subluxation can be due to many different causes, such as:

- Sedentary Lifestyle and Poor Posture
- Traumatic Injuries and Accidents
- Repetitive Motion and Overuse
- Emotional and Mental Stress
- Genetic Predisposition and Congenital Factors[1]

In my work as a chiropractor, I often talk about the spine's alignment as the body's harmony—a way for everything to work together like a perfectly tuned instrument. When I explain vertebral subluxation to my patients, as a lifelong singer, I like to compare it to music.

Imagine an orchestra where one section is out of sync, or a guitar string that's a bit loose. The music still plays, but it sounds off, unbalanced. That's exactly what subluxation does to the body. When one vertebra is out of place, it creates this disconnect in our nervous system, making it harder for our body's "music" to play smoothly. The flow from the brain to every muscle, organ, and tissue is interrupted, and that lack of harmony is where we start to feel discomfort or lose function.

People often think that health means just "no pain," but that's only part of the picture.

People often think that health means just "no pain," but that's only part of the picture. Pain is only about 10% of what the nervous system controls. The other 90% is everything else we don't feel directly—our organ function, our movement, our balance. So, when we wait until pain shows up, it's like waiting for a song to completely fall apart before re-tuning the instrument. Regular adjustments, then, are not about treating pain; they're about keeping that harmony throughout the body, preventing that "off" note from disrupting the whole performance.

This is where people say things like, "Oh, my back started aching out of nowhere, but it didn't seem like a big deal, so I just pushed through," or "I noticed I was spending more nights on the couch, eating more than usual, but I didn't think much of it." Or "I've been working out, but instead of feeling stronger, I'm somehow feeling weaker—no specific injury or anything." We tend to look for those big, obvious moments—car accidents, falls, or major injuries—those clear cause-and-effect events that explain our pain.

But here's the thing: it's often the micro traumas, those small repetitive strains, that are gradually throwing our body out of harmony. It's like one instrument in an orchestra playing just a little off-key. At first, you may barely notice, but over time, the whole song starts to sound "off," even though nothing dramatic happened all at once. These micro traumas build up, shifting us slowly away from harmony.

That's why it's important to pay attention to those small shifts in our "music" before they turn into the big ones that disrupt the harmony altogether.

Think of it as microdosing disharmony into your body. It might not seem like much in the moment, but each little "off note" adds up, creating this big, dissonant effect that eventually disrupts the entire "song" of our body's natural rhythm. Because these shifts happen gradually, they're easy to overlook—until, one day, you realize that your whole system is out of sync, and you're struggling to get back in tune.

All that to say, if you're feeling "off" and can't trace it back to one specific thing, that's a sign. These micro traumas work in the background, quietly adding up. That's why it's important to pay attention to those small shifts in our "music" before they turn into the big ones that disrupt the harmony altogether.

When you don't understand how your body works from within, it's easy to feel out of harmony all the time. But you aren't necessarily out of harmony—you're just out of tune and need some adjusting. Remember how amazed I was when Dr. Yachter looked at my spine and told me the symptoms I had without a word from me? Take a look at the areas of the spine from top to bottom and the symptoms associated with subluxation within each.

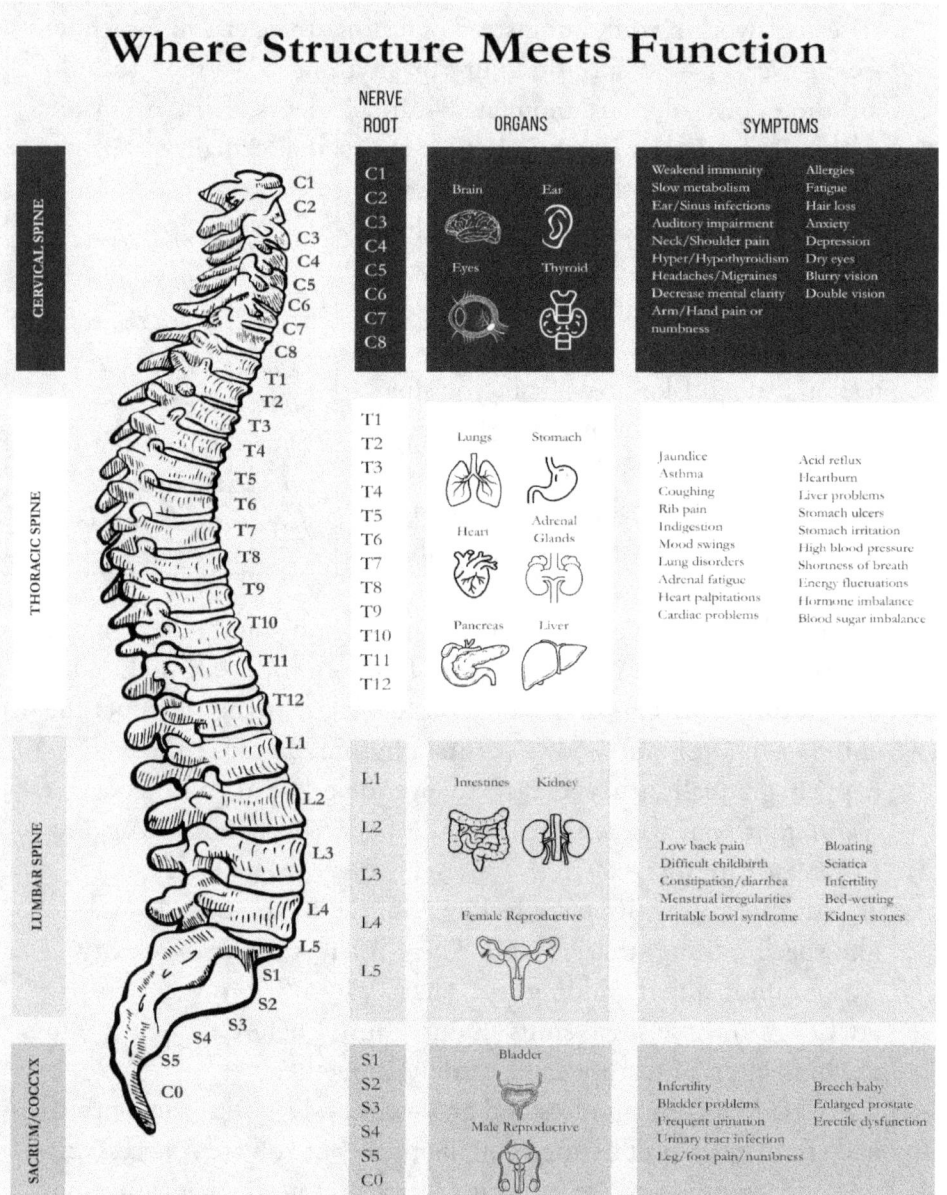

Where Structure Meets Function

CERVICAL SPINE	NERVE ROOT	ORGANS	SYMPTOMS
	C1 C2 C3 C4 C5 C6 C7 C8	Brain, Ear Eyes, Thyroid	Weakend immunity, Allergies Slow metabolism, Fatigue Ear/Sinus infections, Hair loss Auditory impairment, Anxiety Neck/Shoulder pain, Depression Hyper/Hypothyroidism, Dry eyes Headaches/Migraines, Blurry vision Decrease mental clarity, Double vision Arm/Hand pain or numbness
THORACIC SPINE	T1 T2 T3 T4 T5 T6 T7 T8 T9 T10 T11 T12	Lungs, Stomach Heart, Adrenal Glands Pancreas, Liver	Jaundice, Acid reflux Asthma, Heartburn Coughing, Liver problems Rib pain, Stomach ulcers Indigestion, Stomach irritation Mood swings, High blood pressure Lung disorders, Shortness of breath Adrenal fatigue, Energy fluctuations Heart palpitations, Hormone imbalance Cardiac problems, Blood sugar imbalance
LUMBAR SPINE	L1 L2 L3 L4 L5	Intestines, Kidney Female Reproductive	Low back pain, Bloating Difficult childbirth, Sciatica Constipation/diarrhea, Infertility Menstrual irregularities, Bed-wetting Irritable bowl syndrome, Kidney stones
SACRUM/COCCYX	S1 S2 S3 S4 S5 C0	Bladder Male Reproductive	Infertility, Breech baby Bladder problems, Enlarged prostate Frequent urination, Erectile dysfunction Urinary tract infection Leg/foot pain/numbness

Coming in for a Tune Up

When we adjust someone, it's like we're helping their body find its natural rhythm again. They feel relief—not because we're changing their muscles directly, but because we're opening up those channels that let their system move freely and play in harmony. It's not just about that one adjustment; the real healing happens in the space between visits. Each adjustment is like giving the body a fresh tune, a new way to feel "normal," to find its groove again.

As the body starts to settle into these new positions over time, it begins to learn what true harmony feels like, tuning itself a little more each day. It's a gradual shift, but it's powerful. Every adjustment is an invitation for the body to raise its own "volume," to bring out its natural song more fully.

> *It's not just about that one adjustment; the real healing happens in the space between visits.*

Between visits, the body's harmony gets stronger, like practicing an instrument until it sounds just right. I'm excited to share the stories of real people who've rediscovered their rhythm and brought harmony back into their lives. Why don't you put on an honorary doctor's hat as you consider these case studies of some of my real patients? Ask yourself, *What were the cues that their body was already out of tune?*

Emma

Emma came to see me at just three weeks old, and her mom was understandably anxious. Little Emma had been struggling—lots of gas, trouble passing stools, and she wasn't nursing well. Her mom mentioned she could only comfortably turn her head to the left, which made feeding on one side a real challenge. Now, for a newborn, that limited neck movement can make things hard, not just for feeding but for general comfort and function. I immediately recognized that Emma was uncomfortable and likely needed some gentle support to release that tension.

When I examined her, I found that her atlas (the first neck vertebra) was slightly out of alignment, as well as her sacrum, which had a slight rotation. This kind of misalignment is common, and it's amazing how something so subtle can affect a baby so profoundly. Using my adjusting tool—a super gentle instrument tuned for infants—I made specific adjustments to help her body restore harmony. We're not forcing anything; we're simply guiding the body back to a natural, balanced state, allowing the nervous system to do its job and support proper function.

I always ask parents to check in after an adjustment, especially with newborns, so we can see how their little one responds. Within an hour, Emma's mom reached out. She was thrilled to report that Emma had already passed a stool, was sleeping soundly, and seemed so much more at ease. This kind of immediate relief is why I love working with infants—their bodies respond so quickly when given the right support.

This isn't unique to Emma. I see it time and again with my youngest patients. Once the body is in alignment, fussiness eases up, they sleep better, and we start seeing improvements in muscle tone, range of motion, and digestion. It's like watching harmony return to a tiny symphony that was just a bit out of tune. That's the beauty of chiropractic care with infants: restoring balance, helping them find comfort, and setting them up for a healthy start.

Macy

Macy is one of those kids who lights up the room—a little five-year-old ball of energy, sass, and sweetness. When she comes in for an appointment, it's like a mini performance. She struts around the practice, investigating everything with curious eyes, greeting everyone with her own brand of confidence, and even "helping" me adjust her mom. Her mom and I often laugh about how Macy is "five going on twenty-one," with her expressive personality and the way she owns any space she enters. Most days, she's beaming with life, full of joy, and quick to make her presence known.

One day, though, she came in, and it was like her life soundtrack had been silenced. Her mom was carrying her in, which was unusual in itself. Macy was too tired to walk, too quiet to greet anyone, and her usually animated face was pale and drained. Her mom mentioned that Macy had been coughing and seemed unusually lethargic, with none of her usual spark. Even at home, she didn't want to play or do much of anything, which was entirely unlike her. I could see the worry in her mom's eyes—when a little one like Macy suddenly loses her energy, it's unsettling for everyone.

When we got Macy on the table, I could sense how worn down her little body was. I began with her lying face down, using the gentle, specialized tools we have for children. Starting with her lower back, I carefully adjusted her sacrum, then moved up to her mid-back. With children, the focus is always on gentle guidance to bring the body back into alignment, supporting their natural healing processes. Almost immediately after these first few adjustments, her coughing subsided, and there was this noticeable change—she was more relaxed, breathing a bit easier, as if her body could finally start to release the tension it was holding on to.

As I had her turn onto her back, I noticed a little more color returning to her cheeks, and the spark I knew so well seemed to be coming back into her eyes. I then adjusted her atlas, the first bone in the spine, located just under the skull. This area is key because it affects the flow of signals from the brain to the rest of the body, setting the stage for healing. As soon as the atlas is in alignment, it's as if the body's radio is switched back on and the music can play again.

Seeing a child's body restore itself so quickly is one of the most rewarding parts of what I do. With kids like Macy, it's a reminder of how powerful and responsive the body truly is, and how sometimes, all it takes is a little nudge to help them tap back into that natural vitality.

Mary

Mary has been a dedicated client of ours for a while now. As a college professor, she often finds herself sitting for hours, grading exams and dealing with the demands of her role. This grading time is physically taxing, but more than that, it's a point of mental strain for her.

One particular Friday, Mary came in feeling fine physically, but I could sense a familiar cloud of stress hovering over her. She mentioned she was more stressed than usual, but there was no indication of any physical pain. "I just feel tight, Doc," she said. Then, just a few days later, I received an urgent call: she was in severe neck pain, so intense that she couldn't even drive herself to the clinic. When she arrived, she was wearing a neck brace for support—something I'd never seen her use before. Her discomfort had escalated rapidly, and it was clear her body was out of harmony.

During her session, I used my hands and tools to release the tight muscles and gently adjust her spine, all from a seated position since she couldn't lie down. We worked within her limits, bringing balance to her system as best we could. Two days later, she returned feeling about 80% better and, this time, could lay flat on the table. After a full adjustment, she left feeling nearly herself again.

A week later, Mary shared a revelation. She'd felt that familiar tension creeping back in, a signal her body was about to fall out of harmony again. We dug into her triggers, and she realized that stress had crept back in, setting her pace into overdrive. This time, though, she took action—she slowed herself down before her system tipped into full-blown pain.

Mary's story is a powerful example of how our bodies work in harmony with our minds. Her circumstances—the stressors, the workload—didn't change. But she learned to recognize when her body was out of tune and, with this awareness, she could recalibrate before the harmony was lost. It's a beautiful reminder that, with the right self-awareness, we can keep ourselves in balance even in challenging environments.

Katherine

Katherine has been a client of mine for years. I remember early on, after just a week and a half of regular adjustments, she came in with this incredible energy and told me she felt like she could fly. Her body was vibrant, and she was able to tackle everything in her day with ease. But over time, things shifted. She began having trouble holding her adjustments, and instead of that lasting lightness, she'd feel a short-lived boost that quickly faded. Within twenty-four hours, she'd feel drained again, her body out of alignment.

It wasn't until she shared the whole picture—she was raising a special needs child and going through a tough divorce—that the puzzle pieces came together. Katherine's body was carrying so much more than I'd realized, and this was a moment for a community approach. We connected her with a therapist and a coach to walk alongside her, complementing her adjustments. Through this support, she learned how to process her emotions so they wouldn't keep her body's harmony at a low hum.

She made changes, too—adjusting her diet, adding supplements, and creating space for her body to feel strong. Little by little, she was able to tune into her feelings instead of suppressing them. Katherine is still navigating that challenging environment, but now she's equipped to handle it in a way that preserves her energy and keeps her body in tune. This harmony in her mind, body, and spirit has given her a resilience that allows her to thrive, even in the midst of it all.

Abby

Abby, a thirty-three-year-old mom, came to me just worn out, both body and spirit. She was really struggling with her postpartum journey—breastfeeding, feeling connected with her new baby, dealing with aches in her back that wouldn't let up. Holding her daughter was putting strain on her body, especially on her mid-back, and Abby found herself dreading every breastfeeding session because of the pain. She could barely take a deep breath without that sharp ache right in the middle of her back, which had her stuck in this shallow breathing pattern just to avoid the discomfort. As any mom knows, it's heartbreaking to be in so much pain when you're trying to bond with your little one.

Sleep wasn't any better. Abby tried every pillow combination you can think of to get comfortable, but no matter how she arranged things, nothing felt right. Her muscles were so tense and spastic that lying flat just wasn't an option; she had to stack herself up on uneven pillows, hoping for some relief. It was clear her body was way out of balance, and that lack of harmony was taking its toll, leaving her feeling depleted and disconnected from her own motherhood experience.

When Abby finally came in, I found a significant curve in her spine, enough to be diagnosed as scoliosis. With her first session, I focused on gentle corrective spinal techniques to bring some harmony back into her body. As I made the adjustments, you could actually see her face light up with surprise—she shrieked in amazement, feeling the tension release as if it were a weight being lifted. By the time she sat up, she took a deep breath, this time with zero pain. She could breathe fully, feel present, and realize that caring for her baby didn't have to come with pain.

For Abby, this adjustment was more than just physical relief; it was a huge shift in her connection to her baby. No more dread, no more bracing for pain, and no more feelings of guilt for wanting to avoid the discomfort. This was her chance to experience motherhood with ease and joy. When the body is in harmony, the mind and spirit follow, and for Abby, that balance meant she could finally find peace and presence with her baby in her arms.

Dr. Sam

Yes, I'm in here too. You already know a lot about my healing journey, but so many of my patients come to me and I know exactly how they are feeling because I've been right in their shoes.

Just like Abby, when I moved across the country after graduating from chiropractic school and then moved back to Atlanta within six months to establish my practice, all of that change and stress caused me to have shallow breathing as well. Once I received the adjustment my body needed, it released my muscles in a way that I could prosper in health, and I could breathe without pain.

And just like Katherine, I can relate because I, too, have a child with special needs. My older son was born in the COVID era, which kept him from a lot of social interaction as an infant. And come to find out, he is on the autism spectrum and has speech delays. Communication can be a barrier for him; he can go from happily singing to extremely frustrated and crying in seconds. When the episode ends, the intensity of the event can linger with me as his mom and caregiver—ask any mother what it's like dealing with toddler tantrums and they will tell you they felt those emotions in their bones! By the end of the day, I used to fall into my bed the moment after he did.

My motherhood journey began with a lot of stress that my own physical body carried, and each day, I had to get back in tune. I can relate to so many of my clients because at one point in my life, I was one of them: always in pain, unaligned, living in disharmony.

My son is now placed in a class with specialists who understand how to work with him at school while providing therapy, but mom-life has been an eye-opening experience which has led me even deeper into my understanding of the holistic approach needed to care for my clients.

Okay, let's do some doctor-to-honorary-doctor talk. Did you notice some of the patient cues? I noticed the lack of good sleep, the healthy parts of the body overcompensating for the unhealthy parts of the body, the physical misalignment affecting the emotional stress levels. Did you note how all of those micro traumas added up until the patient couldn't take the pain anymore and decided to do something about it? If so, good work my friend; I'm ready to have you join in the fun at my clinic!

As I always tell my patients, "You wouldn't let your favorite song go out of tune, so why let your body?" When we keep the spine aligned and free of subluxations, we're allowing the body to stay tuned, to perform at its best.

Keeping that Music Alive

Life throws all kinds of things at us—stress, injuries, even just the wear and tear of daily routines. All of that pulls us out of alignment, but regular adjustments bring us back to our natural rhythm, our harmony.

Chiropractic care isn't just about cracking bones; it's about restoring flow, synergy, and that underlying balance that makes life feel vibrant and whole.

That's why I'm so passionate about what I do. Chiropractic care isn't just about cracking bones; it's about restoring flow, synergy, and that underlying balance that makes life feel vibrant and whole. Each adjustment is like hitting the reset button, letting the body's natural harmony play uninterrupted. It's about living fully, moving freely, and keeping that music alive within us, day in and day out.

Are you ready to get your life back in tune? The first step is Self-Awareness.

Chapter 3

START WITH SELF-AWARENESS

In any reality, we need to recognize that everything is happening *for* us and not *to* us.

Let that one sink in for a moment.

Now here's another one: we get to *choose* how we want to show up for ourselves and for the people we love. It's just perspective, but perspective can change everything.

Allow me to explain: My beautiful little two-year-old boy needs me to wake him up at 6:30 a.m. if I'm going to get to work on time. Normally, I have a solid fifteen-minute window to get him dressed and into the car so I can make it to work promptly.

> *In any reality, we need to recognize that everything is happening for us and not to us.*

But as you know, life doesn't always serve us the "normal" kind of mornings. So let's talk about one of those abnormal days. (Because sometimes moms run late.)

When I woke him up, he blinked at me sleepily and decided he needed a couple more minutes to stretch, roll around, and let his tiny body transition from cozy dreams to the reality of the day. Finally, he reached up, wrapped his little arms around my neck,

31

and sighed the kind of deep, contented sigh that stops time for a moment. (That part? That part was *everything*.)

"Alright, bud, can you turn off your sound machine for Mommy?" I asked.

He toddled over, sat down halfway there—because apparently, life's tasks are better approached with a brief sit—and sighed again. Then came a sneeze. And a cough. Finally, he turned off the machine and stood up like he'd just completed a heroic mission.

By the time we made it to my room to get him dressed, he was in no hurry to comply. Oh no. He was in an "I'm doing this my way" mode. And of course, I made the rookie mistake of turning off my bedroom light when we were ready to exit. That was clearly his job. He marched back into the room, turned the light back on, and then flipped every light switch he could find just so he could turn them all off again. By then, my fifteen-minute window was not just closed—it was boarded up.

Finally, we headed downstairs. I got him on the changing table, socks and shoes in hand, ready for action. He, on the other hand, had other plans. He spun around with a giddy little glimmer in his eyes and sat up while I made sure he didn't fall off. As I wrestled his first sock on, he handed me a shoe with a grin like he was the manager of the whole operation. I stuffed it under my arm while I got the other sock on, and then he held out one foot at a time as I added a shoe to each one. Once his shoes were on, he proudly tapped the soles together to ensure they passed his very official inspection. "Good to go," he seemed to say.

Of course, we had to wash his hands after they were just tapping the bottoms of his shoes. By the time his hands were clean, he went over to the corner in the kitchen where I keep his stuff. Before he got his supplement, he chose to take his multivitamin gummy out and chew it. I waited for him to carefully chew and swallow his gummy because no one wants to rush a toddler into making them choke. Thirty seconds later, I spoon-fed him his applesauce with his supplements, and then he could have his milk.

By the time we got through breakfast, we were officially behind schedule.

Again, my choice: rush him and lose the moment. *Or*, I could lean in and let it be.

By the time we reached the garage, I made another mistake. I grabbed his jacket and, without thinking, put it beside him in the car, just out of his reach. Cue his tiny but mighty frustration. I got back out of the car, handed him the jacket, and watched his little face beam with satisfaction. Sometimes, *these small wins are everything*.

Here's the thing: each time I saw the clock tick forward, reminding me that I was running later and later, I had a choice. And, friend, on this particular day, I chose my son. I chose to believe this morning was happening *for us*, not *to us*. My son needed a little more time, and I needed to be fully present for him. Work could wait.

When I dropped him off at daycare, he walked in with the biggest, brightest smile. He hugged his friends and ran off to play, ready to start his day with joy. And me? I may have been late, but my little boy was happy, loved, and seen. That is his world. And for this mom? *That is everything*.

You Are Aware and Awake

Did I lose some of you mothers reading that story? Let me be clear, I was not, and am not, always that picturesque example of a patient mother. Sometimes I end up choosing to rush to work like when I have an early client appointment that I can not be late to. My ability to be present in the moment is much harder when outside forces seem to make the choice for me.

You have the power to rewrite, to adjust, to create a narrative that feels harmonious and aligned with who you are becoming.

But that's the thing, *you* are the author of the story of your life. Let that settle in. The pen is in your hand,

and you get to decide how each chapter unfolds. The beauty of this? You have the power to rewrite, to adjust, to create a narrative that feels harmonious and aligned with who you are becoming.

Cultivating self-awareness doesn't have to mean shouting your epiphanies from the rooftops or making grand proclamations to the world. It's not about being perfect or doing the most. In fact, it's simpler than that. If you've made it this far, you are awake enough to realize that you're ready to take steps toward living in harmony, in alignment, with yourself.

Self-awareness is as simple as being present in your daily life. It's about noticing the melody of your days and asking yourself if it sounds right.

Here's the thing: you may not fully understand how your body responds to the subconscious choices you're making every day. You may not see how those quiet decisions ripple through your life—shaping your health, your energy, your joy. But let me tell you, they do. Every choice you make either moves you closer to harmony or pulls you out of sync. So, let's start small.

Self-awareness is as simple as being present in your daily life. It's about noticing the melody of your days and asking yourself if it sounds right. Does it sound like harmony? Or is it off-key in places? No judgment here—just curiosity. Look around, observe, and ask yourself where you might need to fine-tune the balance.

1. *What is on your calendar?*

If you take out your phone and glance at your calendar, it probably tells you all the ways you're busy—meetings, tasks, deadlines, all the noise that fills your day. But let's pause for a moment. What's missing? What part of your life isn't reflected there? Here's the truth: most of us don't schedule *ourselves*. We don't block

When you start your day in alignment, everything else flows from there.

time for our own well-being, and when that happens, life starts to feel off-key—like a song missing its melody, like you're moving but not in harmony with yourself.

Here's the shift: put yourself on the calendar. Seriously. Schedule a moment just for you, the same way you'd prioritize a big meeting or a deadline. It doesn't have to be grand—maybe it's a quiet pause, a few deep breaths, or a moment to set your intentions. That's where harmony begins. When you start your day in alignment, everything else flows from there. The melody of your life starts to sound fuller, more balanced, more *you*. And that's the kind of rhythm you deserve.

2. *How do you wake up in the morning?*

For so many of us, life is what wakes us—the kid crying, a partner saying good morning, or that alarm blaring like it's trying to ruin your day before it starts. But here's the thing: How you wake up matters. It sets the tone for everything else.

Let me ask you this—do you really want to start your day with a sound that shocks your system and makes you jump? Or could something gentler, like birds chirping or chimes swaying in the breeze, help you ease into your morning with a little more harmony? For me, it's birds all the way. Those loud alarms? They make me want to chuck my phone clear across the room. And let me tell you, there's no way I'm trying to wake up feeling immediately annoyed.

When you choose to wake up in a way that feels aligned, you're giving yourself the gift of starting in flow, in harmony.

Now, let's talk about that snooze button. If you're hitting it ten times, you're not waking up with intention, and it's throwing everything off. That kind of start leaves you groggy, out of sync, and chasing energy all day long. But here's the shift: when you choose to wake up in a way that feels aligned, you're giving yourself the gift of starting in flow, in harmony. It's a small choice, but it changes the whole vibe of your day. As Brené Brown reminds us, "practicing gratitude invites joy into our lives," and something as simple as counting backwards from five before opening your eyes—then intentionally naming what you're grateful for—can transform your morning from reactive to reflective, setting the tone for a more grounded, joyful day.[2]

3. How do you go to sleep?

Choose something that keeps your rest as peaceful and aligned as possible.

Sleeping with the television on all night might seem like a good idea for background noise, but let me tell you, it's not doing your subconscious any favors. Think about it—your mind is soaking in whatever's playing, even while you're asleep. And trust me, that's not the harmony your body needs. Instead, let's shift to something more intentional, like a white noise app or a sound machine. Those are designed to help your mind and body rest without all the extra chatter sneaking in.

Now, I've got to warn you—don't go using YouTube as your source for white noise. Why? Because you just might wake up in the middle of the night to someone suddenly talking in your room—only to realize the playlist rolled into a butter ad. (Ask me how I know!) Learn from my mistakes, and choose something that keeps your rest as peaceful and aligned as possible. You'll thank yourself in the morning.

4. What is your gratitude practice?

Gratitude journals are such a beautiful, simple way to tune into the blessings in your life. When you wake up in the morning, you're already blessed with the gift of a new day. Start there. Take a few minutes to jot down three things you're

Gratitude, when shared, becomes harmony in action.

grateful for. Then, when you wind down at night, reflect on the day. Write down three moments, interactions, or experiences that brought you joy or taught you something valuable.

Want to take it a step further? Before you drift off to sleep, set an intention for the next day—something positive for your subconscious to hold on to while you rest. And for bonus points, build some community around your gratitude practice. Ask a friend, partner, or loved one, "What are you grateful for today?" It's such a simple question, but the connection it creates can be powerful. Gratitude, when shared, becomes harmony in action.

5. Where do you find the time?

It's so easy to say we don't have time for things like exercise or building healthy habits. But let's be real—most of us make time for the things we *want* to do. The tricky part is seeing where we can carve out time for the things we *know* we should do. That's where time-tracking comes in.

> The tricky part is seeing where we can carve out time for the things we know we should do.

By tracking your day, you can uncover those hidden pockets of time that might be slipping through the cracks. Maybe it's scrolling on your phone or zoning out in front of the TV. Once you see where those minutes are going, you can create intentional pockets of time for what really matters—moving your body, caring for your health, and aligning with the kind of life you want to live. It's a simple shift, but it's a powerful one. Once you've done this, refer back to number one—schedule this time for you. Stop trying to make it perfect! However it fits into your life is perfect for you. *Harmonize.*

6. *What can you simplify or streamline?*

That's harmony— when your surroundings reflect the peace you're cultivating within.

Have you ever noticed that the more stressed you feel, the more cluttered your house seems to get? It's like a mirror— chaos in your mind shows up as chaos in your surroundings. And while life with kids means things won't ever be *perfect,* you can still create a sense of order by giving everything a place. Trust me, this is something I'm working on myself right now. My home doesn't yet reflect who I've become, and that's okay. I'm in the process of reimagining and reorganizing it to match the peaceful surroundings I want to feel.

There's something so grounding about walking into a space that feels like *you.* A home where the world stays on the other side of the door. I love being able to come inside, take a deep breath, and feel the calm energy wrap around me. That's harmony—when your surroundings reflect the peace you're cultivating within. It's not about perfection; it's about creating a space that feels like home for the version of you that you're becoming.

Connect with Your Chaos

As women, we know all too well that life has a rhythm that shifts— an ebb and flow between calm and chaos that plays out month to month, day to day, and yes, sometimes minute to minute. But what if, instead of trying to fight the chaos or pretend it doesn't exist, you chose to connect with it? Stay with me here. I know that might sound counterintuitive. Why would anyone willingly engage with chaos? Let me explain.

Connecting with your chaos is about acknowledging the unpredictable, messy nature of life instead of denying it. It's recognizing the mix of past experiences, current challenges, and all the little moments in between that shape us. Just like in my chiropractic practice, where we address physical subluxations to restore the flow of energy throughout the body, emotional or energetic subluxations need attention too. Ignoring the chaos doesn't make it disappear. Trust me, anything you push down will eventually bubble back up, often at the worst possible time. When you lean into the chaos instead, observe it, and give yourself grace to process it, you invite harmony to return to your life. Simply put—be present. Your presence will invite the path of healing that you are seeking.

Take my slow-motion morning with my son. It could have gone in a completely different direction. I could've rushed him along, skipped the hug, turned off the lights myself, gotten frustrated when he popped his gummy into his mouth, and maybe even yelled. That frustration could've carried into my day—walking into work late with frantic energy, putting

> *When you lean into the chaos instead, observe it, and give yourself grace to process it, you invite harmony to return to your life.*

my team and clients on edge. Instead, I chose a different perspective. I acknowledged that my son needed me that morning. I leaned into that moment, knowing I'd be late, but also knowing I'd made the right choice for both of us. I admitted to my team and clients why I was late, thanked them for their patience, and we moved through the day with ease. It wasn't perfect, but it was harmonious.

Connecting with your chaos doesn't mean living in a constant state of disorder or inviting chaos in like a houseguest that never leaves. It means accepting that life isn't always neat and tidy, and honestly, it's not supposed to be. Sometimes beauty is in the mess. Chaos, when embraced, can be an opportunity to grow stronger, more present, and more intentional. That's where true harmony begins.

Clarify Your 3 Ts

Let me grab my Dr. Sam hat again and talk about what might be throwing you out of alignment in the first place. When you connect with your chaos, you create space for something powerful—new perspectives, growth, and transformation. It's in those messy, unpredictable moments that you can discover what truly matters and how to realign with your life in meaningful ways.

In my practice, we often address what I call the 3 Ts: *Traumas, Toxins,* and *Thoughts.* These are the forces that disrupt the harmony in our bodies and lives. Traumas—whether physical, emotional, or even generational—can linger and create tension. Toxins, from the foods we eat to the environments we're in, can cloud our systems. And Thoughts, those subconscious patterns or self-doubts, can pull us away from balance. Recognizing these is the first step to reconnecting with yourself and bringing your life back into harmony.

Ready to grab your honorary doctor hat too? Let's dive in.

Traumas

We talked about micro and macro traumas in Chapter Two, and by now, you've probably started to see how those big, obvious events—the macro traumas—affect you differently than the smaller, everyday experiences—the micro traumas—that slowly become out of tune over time.

Here's something we don't talk about enough as moms: pregnancy, childbirth, and breastfeeding are traumas on the body. Yes, they're incredible and life-changing, but they're also physically demanding and emotionally draining. After having a baby, your body is forever changed. And let me tell you, the latest research says it can take up to twenty-four months for your body to begin truly healing. But what do so many of us do?

Once you identify your traumas, you can start the work of processing and healing.

We have another baby before we're fully recovered—because, well, life happens. I've been there, and it's no wonder we end up feeling like we're out of alignment, and we stay in an unharmonious state longer than intended.

Then, as your little ones start moving, it doesn't stop. You're looking down, bending over, constantly picking them up, and holding them on that favorite hip of yours. Over time, all of that affects your posture, your alignment, and ultimately your energy. It's those micro traumas stacking up day after day that quietly pull you out of harmony—physically and emotionally.

Here's the thing: once you identify your traumas, you can start the work of processing and healing. Keeping a traumatic event trapped in your mind, unaddressed, is like carrying a weight that won't let go. Your mind will keep spinning it around and around,

Healing isn't one-size-fits-all.

and it'll show up unannounced when you least expect it. But here's the shift: instead of letting it bounce around, you can process it. Journaling can be a powerful tool—getting those thoughts out of your head and onto paper. Some people prefer recording voice memos to vent their feelings, deleting them afterward as a way to release what's been weighing them down.

And sometimes, you need more support. Working with a professional counselor or therapist can help you go deeper. Listen, finding the right fit in a provider matters. Don't be afraid to take your time, read their bios, or ask for a quick consultation. If they're not the right person, they may know someone who is. Healing isn't one-size-fits-all, but the goal is always the same: restoring harmony, releasing what no longer serves you, and stepping forward into your wholeness. You've got this.

Toxins

Every single one of us has cancer cells living in our bodies—it's a fact, and it's part of how our cells naturally turn over. Whether those cells form tumors depends on a few key factors: the strength of your immune system, how you're managing stress, and what you're putting into your body. This is where harmony comes into play. When your body is out of sync, the balance shifts, and those factors can start working against you. But when you're aligned, your body has the tools it needs to protect and heal itself.

Everything we allow into our lives, whether on our skin, in our food, or in our air, has the potential to support or disrupt our harmony.

Let's start with food, because what you eat changes everything. The pesticides on your fruits and vegetables, the air you breathe, and even the medications you take can impact how your cells develop and regenerate. Cells build tissue, tissue forms muscles and organs, and together, they create the foundation of your body. If you're not giving your body the right nutrients—or if you're taking supplements without knowing what's in them—it can throw your whole system out of harmony. And let me tell you, sometimes the wrong supplement can be worse than taking none at all.

Here's the shift: start being intentional. If you pick up a bottle and can't recognize half the ingredients on the label, pause. That's your body saying, "Hold on, we need to check this out first." Reach out to a certified nutritionist, a functional medical doctor, or someone who knows how to guide you in making choices that align with your body's needs. Harmony starts when you feed your body the right information—through food, through nutrients, and through the products you use every day.

And let's not forget your largest organ—your skin. We put all kinds of things on it, don't we? Lotions, makeup, cleaning products, fragrances—you name it. But here's the deal: toxins from those products can seep through your skin and disrupt the health of your cells. Everything we allow into our lives, whether on our skin, in our food, or in our air, has the potential to support or disrupt our harmony. It's all connected.

If you're ready to take this awareness a step further, there are tools to help. Apps like Think Dirty let you scan barcodes and break down what's really in your products. It's a small shift, but one that puts you in control. Because when you choose products and habits that align with your body's needs, you're not just living healthier, you're creating a life that feels balanced, intentional, and harmonizing in tune.

Thoughts

Our minds control *everything*. The way we think shapes how we behave, how we respond, and ultimately, how we choose to live. And the key word here? *Choose*. Because even when bad things happen—and they will, because life does what it does—*we* still have the power to decide how we interpret those moments and what we do with them moving forward.

Let's sit with this example: you walk into a funeral. The air is heavy, somber, and full of emotions because someone has left this world, and the people gathered are here to support those left behind. As you look around the room, you notice everyone's processing the loss in their own way. Their tears may look the same, but their perspectives? Completely different.

The first person you approach has a calmness about her, a peaceful spirit. After you share a hug, she tells you she's grateful her loved one is no longer in pain. To her, this is a release—a moment of freedom—and she's happy for them, believing they've gone to a better place.

Then you meet the second person. She's trying to smile through her tears but can't hide the furrow in her brow. She's deep in questioning—why this happened, why life has to be so unfair. She's overcome with the thought of how she'll go on without her loved one and clings to the idea that life is too short, asking you to promise to keep in touch more often.

And then there's the third person. She's dabbing her mascara and reminds you of a silly memory you all shared together. You both laugh softly, and before long, you're already planning a new adventure in honor of your lost friend.

Here's the truth: none of these reactions are wrong. Not a single one. They're all reflections of each person's unique perspective and how they're choosing to process their grief. And that's the point—you *choose*. You get to decide if you'll simply accept life as it is or become an active participant in shaping how you respond.

Negative thoughts? They'll come. But if you let them settle in, they can cloud the vision you have for your life. Here's the shift: what if you saw each thought as an observation, not a fact? You'd be able to pause, decide what's worth keeping, and let the rest go. That's where harmony settles in—when you take back your power to shape your mindset and move through life with intention.

Here's the shift: what if you saw each thought as an observation, not a fact?

Consider Where You Are Today

There's something every single one of us craves deep down: a sense of harmony, peace, and connection. It's like the melody that makes life feel whole, complete. The purpose of my work, and everything we're doing here, is to guide you to a place where you can rediscover and revitalize the woman you were always meant to be. As we move forward together, you'll get the chance to dig deeper, to learn more about yourself, and to uncover who you truly desire to be from this moment on. Because let me tell you, child, it's never too late to rewrite your story.

For ten years, I lost my identity. I didn't even realize it at first—I just let it slip away, little by little, as I warped myself to fit into the relationship I was in. When my marriage ended, it was like I woke up and saw how much of my life had been shaped by community decisions. It wasn't about what *I* wanted, what *I* liked, or what *I* believed. There wasn't space for me in my own life. But here's the shift: I decided I was worthy of creating that space. It took work—

still does—but getting reacquainted with myself has been one of the greatest gifts. And if you're reading this, you deserve that too.

An aligned life is an abundant life. It's not about perfection; it's about finding the rhythm that feels right for you. And let me tell you, there are so many ways to start living in alignment, even beyond what we address in my chiropractic practice.

An aligned life is an abundant life.

Time to Reflect

Before we dive into the 6 Cs of Harmony, take a moment to reflect and evaluate where you are right now. Think of this as your baseline—a starting point to measure your progress as you begin to align more fully with the authentic, vibrant version of yourself.

With each question, rate yourself: 1 for never/low, 2 for sometimes/medium, and 3 for always/high. Let's begin.

Physical Health		Mental Health		Energetic Health	
Stretch practice	1 2 3	Feeling sad	1 2 3	Prayer/ Meditation	1 2 3
Sleep quality	1 2 3	Feeling joyful	1 2 3	Personal spirituality	1 2 3
Immune health	1 2 3	Motivation	1 2 3	Mindfulness practice	1 2 3
Caffeine consumption	1 2 3	Control over emotions	1 2 3		
My daily energy level	1 2 3	My daily outlook	1 2 3		

As you reflect on your answers and begin this journey, remember that harmony isn't about perfection—it's about alignment. It's about finding your rhythm, tuning into who you are, and creating space for the woman you're becoming. Each step you take toward understanding yourself brings you closer to a life that feels abundant, balanced, and authentically yours. This is your chance to embrace the process, rediscover your voice, and let your harmony sing.

Chapter 4

CULTIVATE A GROWTH MINDSET

I found out my father passed away while I was at church, after I listened to my friend perform a beautiful solo. Singing had always been a way for me to feel connected—to God, to my community, and, in some ways, to myself. But that day, something felt off. So instead of me performing that reverent act as initially planned, I asked her to step in. I had this sinking feeling in the pit of my stomach that I couldn't shake and I inexplicably began to cry while she was performing. After the service, I had lunch with my family and friends, and forgot that I had not checked my phone in hours.

I saw that my oldest sister had called. Shortly after, my brother called. Then my sister-in-law . . . and immediately knew something was wrong with my father. All of these calls happened at the same time when I found myself crying in the bathroom earlier. The words came out of her mouth, but they didn't feel real. "It's your dad," she said, her voice breaking. "He's gone."

I stood there, frozen, clutching my phone as if holding it tighter could somehow change the words I'd just heard. My chest felt heavy, like I couldn't catch my breath. I ran towards my mother and told her the news and we started the calls that affirmed our deepest sorrows. Everything blurred together in those moments, but the reality was sinking in fast: my dad was gone, and life as I knew it had changed forever.

Life won't always be easy, but you have a choice in how you respond.

I didn't know what to do with myself. One moment, I was standing outside the church, holding my phone like it was a lifeline. The next, I was behind the steering wheel driving myself home—absentmindedly. Grief does that to you—it pulls you out of the present and drags you into a space where nothing feels grounded. In the weeks that followed, I kept asking myself, *"Why? Why did this happen to him? Why now? How could this be happening to me?"* I felt stuck in the pain, drowning in the questions that didn't have answers.

But here's the thing about my dad: he was a teacher even in his absence. As I wrestled with my grief in the months to come, I began to hear his voice in my head, the way he always guided me with his calm, steady wisdom. He used to tell me, *"Life won't always be easy, but you have a choice in how you respond."* That stuck with me.

Slowly, I started to shift my perspective. I realized I couldn't change what had happened, but I could decide how I moved forward. My dad had always been about building strength, not through denial or avoidance, but by facing challenges head-on. His passing became a catalyst for me to think differently, to reshape my mindset, and to find harmony in the chaos.

Mindset isn't about avoiding pain or pretending the hard stuff doesn't exist. It's about making a conscious choice not to stay stuck in that pain. It's about reframing your experiences and aligning your thoughts with the person you want to become. In this chapter, we're going to explore the tools and practices that can help you shift your mindset—whether you're navigating grief, managing stress, or just trying to find balance in your

Mindset isn't about avoiding pain or pretending the hard stuff doesn't exist. It's about making a conscious choice not to stay stuck in that pain.

day-to-day life. Together, we'll learn how to create harmony within ourselves, even in the face of life's greatest challenges.

Tune Your Mind

As you learned back in Chapter Three, you get to choose how you show up in the world. Once you pause, look around, and take stock of your daily life, you open the door to self-awareness. And self-awareness? That's your first step to creating harmony within yourself. Remember, you can't play your best if your body is out of tune.

Your mindset? It's your instrument. It shapes how you see yourself and the world. Let's be honest—it didn't just tune itself overnight. Your mindset is the product of your experiences, beliefs, habits, and how you've responded to life's highs and lows. Since it's taken time to create this melody, it'll take effort to adjust it. And let me be the one to loudly say: *It's possible*. Change the chords, change the song.

Change the chords, change the song.

Here's the thing: we all tend toward either an abundance mindset or one of lack, and these can shift depending on the day (or, let's be honest, the hour). When you're in abundance, you feel it. You move through life like the world is playing your song—shoulders back, head high, making eye contact. You know you're worthy of everything you dream about. But a mindset of lack? That's another story. It whispers, *"I'm not enough,"* or *"Life isn't fair."* And before you know it, you're slouched, gazing at the ground, stuck in the same frustrating refrain. But listen—stuck is a state, not a sentence. You can retune your instrument.

You have the power to reset and realign at any time.

It starts with noticing. Take a moment to tune in. How are you really feeling? What's working? What's out of alignment? That's your body sending you messages. But here's the kicker: self-awareness is the first note, not the whole song. Real transformation happens when you take action. When you consciously realign your thoughts and behaviors, you create the kind of harmony that not only resonates within you, but carries out into every part of your life.

Here's what I need you to know: you have the power to reset and realign at any time. Right now, wherever you are, no matter what's going on. Mindfulness—practicing present-moment awareness without judgment—is how you begin. It's like fine-tuning your instrument so everything plays in balance. When you understand what throws you off-key, you gain the power to shift back into harmony. Little by little, step by step, you create the melody that aligns with who you're truly meant to be.

More Observant, Less Reactive

Triggers are like discordant notes in the song of your life—they stand out, grab your attention, and demand to be addressed. They're the events or observations that stir up emotional or psychological reactions. And here's the thing: understanding when and why you're triggered is one of the most powerful steps you can take toward creating harmony within yourself. It's not always easy, but shining a light on your triggers can help you uncover what's driving your thoughts, feelings, and actions.

When you can acknowledge your triggers, you take back your power. You gain the ability to choose between reacting impulsively or responding consciously. That choice? It's a game-changer. Because let's be honest—reacting on autopilot often leads to a spiral of negative thoughts, actions, and ultimately, a "lack mindset." But when you pause, take a breath, and observe what's happening, it's like stepping back to retune an instrument. Suddenly, you're in control of how the next note plays out.

Understanding when and why you're triggered is one of the most powerful steps you can take toward creating harmony within yourself.

I've learned that when I'm triggered, my body is the first to let me know. My shoulders creep up toward my ears, my chest tightens, and my breathing becomes shallow. Mentally, it feels like someone turned off the lights—I can't think clearly, and everything feels heavier. These physical and mental signals are feedback from your body, telling you, *"Something needs attention here."* When you start to notice those signals, you can stop and ask yourself, *"Why is my body reacting like this?"* That single question can help you step back, observe, and realign.

The key is to become an observer of your feelings rather than identifying with them completely. For example, instead of saying, *"I am angry,"* you might say, *"I feel angry. I wonder why?"* That subtle shift creates space between you and the emotion, giving you room to process and respond. And let's be real—it's not about denying your feelings. It's about recognizing that the emotion is a moment in time, not the whole story.

It's about recognizing that the emotion is a moment in time, not the whole story.

Triggers are like little clues from your subconscious. They're not here to ruin your day; they're here to help you grow. When you notice a big reaction to something, it's worth pausing to ask, *"What is this really about?"* Many times, what feels like a reaction to the present moment is actually tied to something much deeper—something from your past that still needs to be resolved. When you can approach your triggers with curiosity instead of judgment, you create the opportunity to realign and move forward with clarity.

Here's where harmony comes into play. Just as pain in your body signals that something is out of alignment physically, triggers are like emotional dissonance, reminding you to retune. Instead of resisting them or brushing them off, consider them an opportunity to refine your inner melody. They're helping you show up as the person you truly want to be.

I like to use a bird's-eye view when I'm navigating triggers, asking myself questions like:

- Is my safety being threatened in this situation?
- Could there be another explanation for what's happening?
- Can I get clarity before I react?
- If I were a mediator, what would I ask?
- Is this feedback trying to help me grow?
- Is what I'm feeling true, or am I interpreting it incorrectly?
- How can I handle this moment with grace?

No matter how much practice you have with managing triggers, they're going to show up. That's life. The question is, how do you want to respond when they do? I like to ask myself, *"Is my capacity wide enough right now to handle this with grace?"* If it's not, I take a moment to breathe, reset, and choose my next move intentionally.

Even in high-stress situations, I've learned how to flip the script. For example, having a long list of clients can feel overwhelming if I let it. But instead of seeing it as chaos, I remind myself that this is a sign of growth—it's an indication that everything is working in my favor. When I shift my mindset, I can approach my work with gratitude and energy, pouring into my clients and team without feeling drained. On those days, I leave with a spring in my step, knowing I've shown up as my best self and created a positive impact.

The beauty of working through triggers is that it helps you shift from reacting to leading. It allows you to proactively align your mindset with the life you want to create. When you start to see triggers as feedback, not interruptions, you can create the harmony you've been looking for. And let me tell you, living in

Is my capacity wide enough right now to handle this with grace?

tune with your highest self? It's worth every pause, every question, and every intentional step forward.

Slow Down and Breathe

When you think of mindfulness and breathwork, what image comes to mind? Is it someone sitting completely still on a yoga mat, eyes closed, peaceful expression, with nowhere to be and nothing else to do? Sure, that's one way to do it. On a retreat I attended with a dear friend, I experienced a practice that looked a lot like that—a serene, tranquil space where we were guided to focus inward and tune in to our breath. It was beautiful, restorative, and just what I needed in that moment. But what I learned afterward, and what was even more powerful, was how those same techniques can work in real-life situations—the messy, unpredictable ones where life doesn't slow down for a yoga mat.

Your breath is a tool you can use anytime, anywhere, to help you respond rather than react. Shortly after the retreat, I had an opportunity to put this into practice during a business meeting. A colleague made a comment that triggered me—one of those comments that stings, not because of what was said, but because of what it stirred up in me. My first instinct was to react, to say something sharp in return, to defend myself. But instead, I remembered the power of the pause.

At that moment, I told myself, *"You have a choice."* I decided to say, "Let me think about it." Then I gave myself eight seconds to just breathe. In for four counts, out for four counts. That small act—a single breath cycle—was enough to give me space to process my emotions and gain control over my initial reaction. When I responded, it came from a place of clarity and calm rather than defensiveness. The conversation moved forward in a way that felt productive, and I walked away feeling proud of how I had handled it. That eight-second pause made all the difference.

Your breath is like a bridge between your conscious and subconscious mind. It connects the two systems in your body that are responsible for your reactions: the sympathetic and parasympathetic nervous systems. When you gasp in fear or surprise, you're tapping into your sympathetic nervous system—the one that triggers your fight-or-flight response. On the other hand, when you exhale that long "ahhh" of relief after a refreshing sip of lemonade on a hot day, you're activating your parasympathetic nervous system, which promotes relaxation. By consciously regulating your breath, you can harmonize these two systems, creating space to shift from an instinctual reaction to an intentional response.

Here's the truth: there is no urgent clock forcing you to react to everything immediately. That's one of the best lessons I've learned. You always have the time to pause, breathe, process, and make a choice. Whether it's a tense conversation in a meeting, an email that rubs you the wrong way, or even an unexpected comment from someone you trust, you can slow down and take control of how you respond.

You always have the time to pause, breathe, process, and make a choice.

For example, let's talk about emails. Have you ever read an email that made you want to fire off a response right away? I've been there. One of my favorite strategies is to write a first draft—unedited and unaddressed—that I never intend to send. Once it's out of my system, I delete it, walk away, and come back to it later with fresh eyes. Sometimes it takes two, three, even four drafts before I feel ready to hit send. And you know what? That final version is always better—more thoughtful, more constructive, and a lot more aligned with the person I want to be.

The same principle applies to everyday conversations. Tapping into a "waiting clock" for just a few seconds can make all the difference. Those eight little seconds of breathwork are often all it takes to turn a reactive moment into a mindful one. It's a way of creating harmony in your interactions and ensuring that what you put into the world reflects your best self.

Breathwork isn't just about managing stress or navigating difficult moments. It's about reclaiming your power and creating a sense of calm in the chaos. Every time you pause, you're giving yourself the gift of clarity—the space to process your emotions and choose how you want to respond. When you slow down and breathe, you're not just resetting your mindset; you're tuning your inner harmony so you can show up in the world the way you want to.

Victim to Victor

There are moments in life that knock the wind right out of us. Those moments where you find yourself asking, *"How could this possibly be happening for me?"* And let's be real—it doesn't feel like it's happening *for* you. It feels like it's happening *to* you. In those moments, it's so easy to get stuck in the loop of *what happened.* That's when unforgiveness, worry, fear, anxiety, or even depression can creep in, setting up camp in your mind. Your body follows suit—your shoulders tense, your posture becomes rigid, and your mind feels boxed in, unable to see beyond the walls of what just happened.

Here's the truth: when you're stuck in that protective space—keeping the doors closed, the windows locked—you might feel safe, but you're not really living. Sure, you've shut out the pain and risk of more hurt, but you've also shut out the possibility. You're closed off to new experiences, new opportunities, and new joys. The box feels familiar, even comfortable in a way, but it also keeps you small. And being stuck in that small, guarded space can make it hard to see yourself as anything but a victim of your circumstances.

So how do you shift from feeling like a victim to stepping into your power as a victor? It starts with reframing your mindset. You remind yourself—over and over again, if needed—that everything happens for you. Now, let me stop you there, because I know exactly what you're thinking: *"How could this be for me? I didn't choose this. I didn't ask for it. I didn't want it."* That resistance? It's valid. You don't have to pretend it didn't happen or that it wasn't hard.

Acknowledging what happened and how you feel about it is part of the process. But here's the secret: you don't have to let it define you.

When we hold on to a victim mentality, it's easy to believe that being a victim means we're weak. But being a victim doesn't mean weakness—it means something happened to you. That's it. The choice to stay in that mindset or step into your power as a victor? That's entirely yours. It's not about pretending the event didn't happen or that it didn't hurt; it's about deciding whether or not you let it control your future.

Let me give you an example. Imagine a woman who was attacked and robbed at gunpoint. She's shaken, terrified, and unsure of how to move forward. In an effort to feel strong, she signs up for a kickboxing class. She wants to protect herself, to make sure it never happens again. From the outside, it looks like she's stepping into her power, but inside, she's still holding on to the belief that she's a victim. That belief keeps her tethered to fear. So how does she truly shift into feeling like a victor?

First, she separates her body from her soul. Her body went through something traumatic—that's undeniable. But that trauma doesn't have to break her spirit. She recognizes that what happened wasn't her fault; it wasn't about what she was wearing, what she said, or what she did. Someone else made a choice, and while she couldn't control their actions, she can control how she chooses to move forward. She starts seeing her kickboxing class not just as a way to protect herself, but as a way to rebuild her confidence, feel stronger in her body, and reconnect with her power. Over time, she might even use her experience to support other women, becoming a beacon of resilience and strength.

Here's the thing: finding the good in a bad situation is hard. Sometimes, it feels impossible. When my father passed away, I couldn't see how that loss could ever be "for me." I love him. I miss him every single day. I want him here with me. But as time went on, I began to see the lessons he left behind—the way he parented, the example he set, the mistakes he admitted and the ones I learned from on my own. I could take those lessons and carry them forward.

I could choose a partner who reflected the kind of father I wanted for my children. I could honor his memory by using what he taught me to grow. Slowly, I began to see how even that heartbreaking loss could help shape me into the person I am today.

This kind of mindset shift doesn't happen overnight. It's a process, and it takes work—sometimes with a professional, sometimes with a trusted friend or mentor who can hold space for you. It's about asking yourself, *"How can I use this experience for good?"* Maybe you honor a loved one by starting a foundation in their memory that helps others. Maybe you share your story to encourage someone else. Or maybe you simply allow yourself to heal and find strength in the person you're becoming.

Moving from victim to victor doesn't mean pretending everything is fine. It means taking what life hands you and using it to create something beautiful. It's about stepping out of that box, opening the window a crack, and letting in a little light. It's about creating harmony in your life—not by erasing the pain, but by weaving it into a story of resilience, growth, and hope. And let me tell you, when you step into that harmony, you'll feel it deep in your soul. You're no longer just surviving—you're thriving. That's what it means to go from victim to victor.

Give Yourself GRACE

Let's be honest, life can be chaotic. Some days, it feels like the world is pulling you in ten different directions at once. That's why it's so important to ask yourself: *"What am I doing to take care of myself— mentally, physically, and spiritually—on a regular basis?"* Because here's the thing: taking care of yourself isn't selfish; it's foundational. The way you show up for yourself sets the tone for how you show up for everything and everyone else.

One of the simplest ways to start is by committing to caring for yourself, whatever that looks like for you. Every time a client walks through our practice doors, I love to remind them of this. I'll say, "Hey, great job being intentional and making time for YOU today."

It's a small thing, but it matters. You've got to celebrate yourself for showing up, because let's face it, life gets busy, and prioritizing your own well-being is something to be proud of.

Taking care of yourself isn't selfish; it's foundational.

We even have a t-shirt at the office that says, *"I'm sorry for what I said before my adjustment."* It's funny, sure, but it's also a reminder of just how connected our physical and mental alignment are. When you're aligned—body, mind, and spirit—it's so much easier to be your *true* self. That's why my team and I make it a priority to look at every person who walks through our door with nothing but love. Sometimes, the attitudes we see are simply a reflection of the pain they're carrying—physical, emotional, or otherwise. But when they leave a little more aligned, it's incredible how their energy shifts.

Creating alignment doesn't have to be complicated. It starts with simple, consistent habits that help you cultivate mindfulness and reconnect with yourself. And when you feel like your mindset is slipping, remember to give yourself *GRACE*.

Gratitude

Gratitude has a way of shifting your focus from what's missing in your life to what's already here. It's about noticing the good—the people, experiences, and opportunities that bring joy and richness to your world. And let me tell you, gratitude isn't about the big, flashy moments. It's about the little things. Keep a notebook by your bed and write down three things you're grateful for before you go to sleep. In the morning, jot down three things you're excited about or three people who make you feel blessed. These small rituals might seem simple, but they can have a big impact on your mindset. Gratitude is the

Gratitude is the ultimate perspective shifter—it creates harmony in your heart by grounding you in what's good.

ultimate perspective shifter—it creates harmony in your heart by grounding you in what's good. You'll find yourself in search of things throughout your day that you can be grateful for and to celebrate by the end of the day.

Reconnect to Your Purpose

Let's talk about your "why." What is it that drives you? What lights you up? Reconnecting with your purpose is about going deeper than just the material rewards—it's about aligning your values with your actions. When you're living in alignment with your purpose, that's when you feel that deep, abundant happiness that fills you up from the inside out. It's not about checking boxes or earning more things; it's about living authentically. When you're aligned with your purpose, everything else starts to flow.

Accept Responsibility

Here's the truth: you are the author of your life story. That means you have the power to choose how you show up every single day. Accepting responsibility doesn't mean blaming yourself for everything—it means owning your choices and realizing that you have the power to steer your life in any direction you want. When you embrace this truth, you step into your power. You stop seeing yourself as a passive participant in your life and start showing up as the creator of your own path.

You stop seeing yourself as a passive participant in your life and start showing up as the creator of your own path.

Cycles of Positivity

The energy you surround yourself with matters. When you intentionally feed your mind with positivity, you expand your capacity for hope, resilience, and optimism. For me, this changes day to day. Some mornings, I'll listen to a sermon that helps me realign my spirit. Other times, I'll turn to an inspiring podcast or just play a playlist that lifts my mood. The key is to be honest with yourself about what you need in the moment and make it a habit to bring positivity into your day in a way that resonates with you. You don't have to overthink it—just find what works and lean into it. Don't sit in overwhelmed limbo and create paralysis analysis. Try one thing and see how it helps, and if it doesn't, move down the list and keep trying.

Enduring Presence

Let's get real for a second. Life is happening all around you, and you miss it when you're glued to your phone or grinding nonstop for the next big thing. I've seen clients who put their careers and money above everything else, only to end up with broken bodies and empty souls. Let me tell you something: no amount of money is going to fix your spirit. *Presence is vital.* Being present allows you to see what really matters—the beautiful moments right in front of you. It's about slowing down enough to take stock of the things that truly bring you joy and fulfillment. When you're present, you create space for harmony in your life.

When you embody the principles of GRACE, you're giving yourself permission to realign. You're nurturing a proactive approach to self-care, mindfulness, and wellness. It's not about perfection—it's about progress. GRACE helps you cultivate a mindset of abundance, reconnect to your purpose, and move through your days with resilience and strength. And here's the best part: when you give yourself GRACE, you're better equipped to extend it to others. That's the ripple effect of living in harmony with yourself.

Presence is vital.

Meditation for Beginners

Now, before you start worrying about creating some elaborate, picture-perfect meditation practice, let me remind you of something: meditation begins wherever you are, just as you are, right now. There's no right or wrong way to start. Just like any journey, the best way to begin is to do exactly that—begin. Start small. Start messy. Start imperfectly. Just start.

When I first tried meditation, I wasn't sitting cross-legged on a yoga mat in a candlelit room. Far from it. My practice began in my car, during my lunch break, with a free guided meditation app I found on my phone. I sat there in the parking lot, closed my eyes, and followed along as a calming voice led me through a series of visualizations. I didn't do it perfectly—my mind wandered, and I had to keep pulling myself back to the present moment. But you know what? It felt good. It felt like pressing pause on the chaos of my day and giving myself the gift of a little extra care. That's all meditation really is: a moment to realign with yourself and create a sense of harmony in your inner world.

For beginners, meditation apps are an incredible tool. You don't need anything fancy—no special equipment, no secluded space. You can meditate wherever you are: in your car, at your desk, in bed, or even during a quick five-minute walk to the water cooler and back. The most important part isn't how you do it; it's simply your willingness to commit to the practice. That's what matters most. The more you show up, the more you'll begin to feel the benefits.

If you're not sure where to start, keep experimenting with different apps until you find one that resonates with you. Each guide has their own unique style, and finding a voice that feels right for you can make a huge difference. Having someone guide you through the practice allows you to surrender control, quiet your mind, and simply *be*. Most guided meditations will start by focusing on your breath, and as you've learned, your breath is a powerful tool for slowing down triggered thoughts and emotions. It's like hitting the reset button in your mind.

The beauty of meditation is that it's versatile. You can tailor your practice to meet whatever need you have at the moment. Want to feel more energized? There's a meditation for that. Looking to relax and unwind? There's one for that too. Need to calm your mind before bed? You can find meditations designed to help you drift off to sleep. Whether you need five minutes to reset at your desk or a longer session to deeply restore your energy, there's an option for you. It's all about finding what works for you.

Once you find something that feels right, start creating a routine. Add meditation into your daily rhythm, like brushing your teeth or making your morning coffee. You don't have to overthink it—just find a time that works for you and show up. Over time, those small moments of mindfulness will start to stack up, creating a ripple effect in your life. You'll notice you feel calmer, more centered, and more in tune with yourself.

Meditation isn't about perfection—it's about progress. It's about carving out time to connect with yourself, quiet the noise of the world, and realign with the harmony within you. And the best part? You don't have to wait for the "perfect" moment to start. Start now. Start wherever you are. Start messy. Just start. And watch how those small, simple moments of stillness create a big impact in your life.

Flip Your Mindset

Shifting your mindset from negative to positive isn't something that happens overnight. It's a journey—a daily practice of catching those moments when you feel off balance and realigning yourself with the harmony you want to create in your life. I'm not saying it's always easy, but I can tell you it's always worth it. And here's the good news: there are so many ways to flip your mindset when you feel stuck. Let me share some of my favorite strategies with you, ones that have worked wonders in my life and that I turn to again and again.

1. Change the Narrative: Your thoughts create your reality, and the stories you tell yourself matter. When you're feeling less than your best, affirmations can be a powerful tool to rewrite those stories. But here's the trick—you can't just say them, you've got to *feel* them. For example, if the affirmation is, *"I am worthy,"* look at it, say it out loud, and then agree with it: *"I am worthy. Yes, I am worthy."* Feel the truth of those words. Let them settle into your heart. This creates an internal cycle of affirmation that you can come back to any time you need a quick mindset reset. The more you practice, the more these positive narratives start showing up in your life.

> *It's about carving out time to connect with yourself, quiet the noise of the world, and realign with the harmony within you.*

Listen, I get it. You may find it hard to believe these affirmations at first. This is where you may benefit from the professional help of a therapist or a coach to explore the reason behind your negative narratives in order to work through those feelings and thoughts. Just as easily as the negative thought enters, remember you can choose at that moment to switch it.

For example, if you wake up with the thought of, "I am tired, I don't want to go to work." Immediately start speaking against those thoughts (yell if you have to), and change the story. "Today is going to be a great day, I have slept enough to conquer the day, and I will be productive and profitable."

Say it over and over again and start smiling in acknowledgement. Say it with your inner and outer voice. Feel the vibration of the words throughout your body as you do. Then go make it your best day. All you have is now.

2. Shift Your Mood with Music: There's nothing like the right song to shift the energy in a room—or inside of you. Music has the power to uplift, energize, and even heal. When you feel your mindset dipping into negativity, ask yourself: *What kind of music makes me feel alive?* Create playlists for different moods. I have a "motivational playlist" that I turn to when I need to feel unstoppable and inspired, and a "chill playlist" for when I want to settle my energy and refocus.

And don't stress about making the "perfect" list—just start with five songs that lift your mood and add to it when inspiration strikes. Those songs can become an anchor for you when you need to flip your mindset in a hurry.

3. Learn from Motivational Content: Sometimes, when I'm in a rut, I lean into the wisdom of others to help me shift. There was a month in my life when I lived in the *Elevation Church with Steven Furtick* series of sermons. I listened to them in the car, at home— basically everywhere. There were moments when his words felt like they were meant just for me, like they were reaching right into my heart and saying, *"Keep going."* Motivational content like podcasts, books, or sermons can be a lifeline when you need encouragement. Create a list of your go-to resources and turn to them when you need a reminder that you can push forward. Sometimes, hearing someone else's perspective is all it takes to reignite your own spark.

4. Take a Moment to Step Away: Let me say this loud and clear: it's okay to take a break. We've all had those moments when the best thing we can do is walk away for a bit. Whether it's stepping out to grab a drink of water, taking a quick walk to the restroom, or finding a quiet space to sit and breathe, separating yourself for just a few minutes can work wonders. One of my favorite tools is my five-minute water break. I'll leave my office, grab some water, and listen to a short meditation while I'm away. When I return, I feel more grounded and ready to tackle whatever's next. Sometimes, it's those little moments of separation that help you reset and find your flow again.

5. Pay Attention to Your Body: Your body is always talking to you—are you listening? When your body feels tight, tense, or restrictive, that's your cue to stretch. Even if you're at work, you can go do morning stretches to loosen up areas that need attention. Movement creates space, not just in your body, but in your mind. By releasing that physical tension, you're also releasing the mental strain that often comes with it. Remember, harmony starts from within, and that includes how you feel in your body.

Harmony starts from within, and that includes how you feel in your body.

6. Write It Out: When your thoughts are spinning in circles, creating chaos and making it hard to focus, writing can be a lifesaver. Grab a notebook and pour it all out—every worry, every frustration, every scattered thought. Once it's on paper, you can step back and look at it objectively. Ask yourself: *Why are these thoughts showing up? What are they trying to tell me?* Writing clears your mental space, giving you room to focus on more constructive, empowering ideas. It's like a mental decluttering session, and trust me, the clarity you gain is worth it.

Flipping your mindset isn't about ignoring the hard stuff or pretending everything is fine. It's about finding tools and practices that help you move through the tough moments with more grace, more ease, and more alignment with the person you want to be. Whether it's music, movement, affirmations, or just stepping away for a moment, you have so many ways to bring yourself back to a place of harmony. And when you do, you'll notice the shift—not just in your mind, but in how you show up in the world. That's the power of mindset work. That's the power of choosing harmony, every single day.

Make Space for Growth

Remember, I get it—life is hard. Some days it feels like the world is asking too much of you, and it's okay to admit when you're having a tough time. There's no shame in saying, *"I'm struggling right now,"* or acknowledging when you're feeling stuck. In fact, that acknowledgment is a powerful first step. It's an act of self-awareness, and it's part of the process of creating harmony within yourself.

But here's the key: while it's important to honor those feelings, it's equally important to make the conscious choice not to stay there. You can't shove those feelings down and expect them to disappear—they'll only resurface later, often louder than before. Instead, give yourself permission to feel them, explore them, and then decide how you want to move forward. That's where your power lies. When you choose to process your emotions rather than burying them, you're making room for healing, growth, and alignment.

> *While it's important to honor those feelings, it's equally important to make the conscious choice not to stay there.*

This isn't about pretending everything is fine or forcing yourself to "be positive" when you're not feeling it. It's about holding space for your emotions while also holding on to the belief that you're capable of moving through them. *That's the harmony we're working toward*—the balance between acknowledging where you are and taking steps toward where you want to be. It's about showing up for yourself, even on the hard days, and remembering that every moment is an opportunity to realign with the person you're becoming.

As we move forward, we're going to dive deeper into this idea. We'll talk about the importance of *Cherishing Your Emotions*—all of them. Yes, even the hard ones. Because when you learn to Connect with Your Emotions, you're not just surviving—you're thriving. You're creating space for compassion, clarity, and connection, both with yourself and with the people around you. Together, we'll explore how embracing your emotional world can help you live a life that's not just in tune, but truly harmonious. Let's keep going.

Chapter 5

CONNECT WITH YOUR EMOTIONS

On some level, I knew my divorce was inevitable. It didn't happen overnight. It wasn't a single event or a dramatic fallout; it was a slow unraveling. I had been living in survival mode for so long, pushing through, ignoring the signs.

For a year, my husband and I were in therapy, together and separately, trying to make sense of what was left of our marriage. My days were consumed by my growing practice, and my nights were a blur of frustration, sadness, and anger while I navigated newborn life. I felt myself shifting, pulling further and further away from him. It didn't help that I gave birth to my oldest son a couple days after the Covid-19 outbreak rose to pandemic level. That created further uncertainty and isolation. This did not mix well with my business/family dynamic, and the stress upon our marriage was tremendous.

Remember my mantra? *"It is what it is . . . Until it's not."* I wanted things to work, but sometimes, wanting isn't enough.

That June of 2021, it was clear we couldn't go on. We separated. I signed what I thought were the final divorce papers in July. Then, in August, life threw me the biggest curveball: I was pregnant. The rollercoaster of emotions was unlike anything I had ever experienced. One minute, I was grieving the loss of my marriage; the next, I was grappling with what it meant to bring another life into the world on my own. There were moments I felt like I couldn't catch my breath.

Sadness and anger were constant companions, but I didn't have the time—or maybe the courage—to fully sit with them. Instead, I threw myself into my work and single motherhood. My practice was thriving, my babies were growing, but I was shrinking. It's funny how you can look so "successful" on the outside but feel like you're crumbling on the inside. My energy was zapped, and I felt like I was dragging myself through each day. I knew I was ignoring my body. I mean, I tell my clients all the time, "Your body keeps score," but I wasn't keeping up with my own. The signs were all there—the tightness in my chest, the ache in my hips, the exhaustion I couldn't shake.

It's funny how you can look so "successful" on the outside but feel like you're crumbling on the inside.

By the second trimester, I realized I couldn't keep pushing through. My body wasn't going to let me. I developed gestational diabetes, something I know was a direct result of not taking care of myself consistently. The heartburn I'd experienced during my first pregnancy was back, but this time it was worse. And then there were the panic attacks—sudden, overwhelming moments that left me feeling like I was drowning. It was like my body was screaming at me to slow down, but I didn't know how. I didn't want to face what was really going on.

The tightness in my chest turned into pain in my hips. For me, it always ends up in the hips. That's where I carry my stress, my sadness, my anger—all the things I'm not ready to let go of. With my first pregnancy, I dealt with debilitating pelvic dysfunction. This time, the pain wasn't as severe, but it was there, lurking, waiting for me to acknowledge it.

Back then, I didn't feel like I had the space to really process anything. I didn't know how to talk about what I was feeling, and I wasn't ready to hear what my husband had to say either. I just wanted to express my emotions without having to absorb his. But instead of saying anything, I held it all in. "People wouldn't understand,"

I told myself. That's the story I clung to, and it kept me silent. It's cultural, in some ways. Growing up, I learned to keep things quiet. "Don't air your dirty laundry." And so, I didn't.

But holding it all in came at a cost. I wasn't eating enough, and when I did eat, I wasn't paying attention to what my body actually needed. My blood sugar numbers climbed, and I developed gestational diabetes. The guilt hit me hard. I knew better. I should've done better. But guilt isn't helpful when you're trying to survive.

Six months into my pregnancy, my belly had grown, and so had the clarity. The marriage was over. There was no salvaging it. I couldn't look to my ex for closure or healing—I had to figure it out on my own. That was when the shift started. I began paying attention to my health, one small step at a time. I ate more consistently, which helped me manage my blood sugar without needing medication. I started listening to my body in ways I hadn't before, and slowly, I began to feel more like myself.

What I've learned through all of this is that the body doesn't lie.

When my son was born, healthy and on his due date, it felt like a small victory. But I knew the work wasn't done. Healing takes time, effort, and intention, and I wasn't anywhere close to "done." Even now, I'll admit, it's still a work in progress. But I'm miles away from the person I was back then.

What I've learned through all of this is that the body doesn't lie. When we ignore our emotions, our body holds on to them, and it will find ways to make us listen. For me, it showed up in my chest, my hips, my blood sugar. For someone else, it might be headaches, fatigue, or muscle tension. But the truth is always there, waiting for us to notice it. I see it in my patients all the time, and now, I see it in myself.

Healing isn't about perfection. It's about progress. It's about learning to tune in to what your body is telling you and finding ways to care for yourself, even in the middle of chaos. I used to think everything had to be fixed immediately, but I've realized that it's okay to take it one step at a time. It's okay to say, "This is enough for today," and try again tomorrow.

It's about learning to tune in to what your body is telling you and finding ways to care for yourself, even in the middle of chaos.

Fast-forward to today, and I can look back with gratitude. Gratitude for the lessons, for the growth, and for the tools I've gained along the way. My experiences didn't just happen to me—they happened for me. They've made me stronger, more compassionate, and more connected to the person I want to be. And while I'm still learning, I know one thing for sure: I'll never stop showing up for myself, for my boys, and for the life I deserve.

Ignored Emotions Don't Go Away

Here's the thing about emotions: they don't disappear just because you're not ready to deal with them. We think we can "keep it moving," bury the pain, and push forward. Throw yourself into work, keep busy, stay distracted—believe me, I've been there. But ignoring emotions doesn't mean they go away. They stay, buried just below the surface, waiting for the right moment to demand your attention. Or, more likely, they show up in ways you don't expect. It's like I always say: "Your body remembers everything, even the things your mind tries to forget."

Sigmund Freud said it well: "Unexpressed emotions will never die. They are buried alive and will come forth later in uglier ways." Maybe you've felt this. One minute, you're fine, everything seems normal, and then out of nowhere, anger, sadness, or frustration bubbles up over something so small it doesn't even

Your body remembers everything, even the things your mind tries to forget.

make sense. Like when someone cuts you off in traffic and then gets stuck at the same red light as you. It's not about the driver—it's about something deeper. Or maybe you're watching a movie, and the way a character shifts their feet or runs their fingers through their hair reminds you of someone you've lost. Before you know it, you're crying, and you don't even fully understand why.

These moments aren't random. They're signals. Your body is asking you to slow down, acknowledge what's there, and give those buried emotions the space to surface. It's uncomfortable, but it's necessary. Because if you don't, those emotions will find other ways to live in your body. They'll show up as pain in your back, tightness in your chest, or a racing heart you can't seem to calm.

I learned this the hard way when my father passed away during my college years. My father—gone. Just like that. It was like the ground had been pulled out from under me. But instead of stopping to grieve, I told myself, "I have to stay on track." Within a week, I was back in class, acting like nothing had happened, trying to pretend I was okay. I thought I could outwork my grief, outrun it, and keep it from catching up with me. I was wrong.

The truth is, my father's death was everywhere. Every memory of him was magnified, waiting for me around every corner. I would tell myself, "I don't have time for this," and keep pushing forward, but grief doesn't wait for permission. It shows up when it's ready, not when you are. I'd be out with friends and suddenly feel overwhelmed, out of nowhere. A song would play, or someone would say something, and all the feelings I'd been trying to bury would rush to the surface. I'd feel like I couldn't breathe, but I still didn't let myself fully stop.

One moment in particular still stays with me. It was the first year my father wasn't there for his birthday, and I just couldn't keep it together. I kept thinking about him. About the sacrifices he made, about the hustle I'd seen him live every day of his life, and about how I was repeating the same pattern—working through my pain instead of feeling it. I didn't give myself the space to process his absence, and it showed up in ways I didn't expect.

Growing up, my father was a force. He worked so hard, too hard, always juggling multiple jobs, businesses, and responsibilities.

He wanted to give us everything he didn't have, but the cost of that hustle was high. Even when he was home, he was often somewhere else in his mind—thinking about the next project, the next move, the next way to provide. But the moments when he was fully present? Those were gifts. I remember sitting with him as a child, watching him laugh or tell a story, and feeling like all was right in the world. Those memories are precious, and they're part of why losing him hit me so hard. It wasn't just losing my dad—it was losing the possibility of ever having more of those moments with him.

When I talk about harmony, this is what I mean. Harmony isn't about erasing pain or pretending it doesn't exist. It's about letting all the parts of your life—joy, grief, anger, hope—live together without drowning each other out. My father's life taught me that misalignment has consequences and that the concept of balance was just that: a hypothesis, a scientific objective that wouldn't prove practical as the scales will remain tipped. He worked until his body couldn't keep up anymore, and it caught up with him in the end. I see so much of him in myself—his drive, his determination, his resilience—but I also see the cost of not making time to rest, to process, to feel. I don't want to repeat that.

It's about letting all the parts of your life—joy, grief, anger, hope—live together without drowning each other out.

It took me years to understand that I couldn't outwork my emotions. No matter how much I tried, the grief didn't go anywhere. It stayed in my body, taking up space until I finally gave it the attention it deserved. For me, the emotions often lived in my chest, like a weight pressing down, making it hard to breathe. Other times, they showed up in my hips, that familiar ache reminding me of everything I was holding on to. My body kept asking me to slow down, to process, to listen.

Eventually, I started to. I learned that grief isn't something you "get over." It's something you carry. But you don't have to carry it alone, and you don't have to carry it all at once. I gave myself permission to feel—to cry when I needed to, to talk about my father and the memories we shared, to let go of the guilt I'd been holding on to for not stopping sooner. And as I did, I began to heal.

Now, when I talk to my patients, I tell them the same thing I had to tell myself: "Your body isn't your enemy. It's your greatest ally, and it's always trying to tell you something." The pain you feel, the tension, the exhaustion—they're messages. They're asking you to slow down, to pay attention, to honor what's happening inside of you. Ignored emotions don't go away—they take up residence in your body, and they'll stay there until you're ready to deal with them.

So whatever you're carrying, know this: it's okay to take your time. It's okay to feel it all, even when it feels overwhelming. Healing isn't about being perfect—it's about being honest, with yourself and with your body. The only way out is through, and the more you allow yourself to process what's there, the freer you'll feel. Trust me—I've been

I learned that grief isn't something you "get over." It's something you carry.

there, and I've learned that when you listen to your body, it will always lead you back to yourself.

Ignored Emotions Become Stored Emotions

Let's put on my Dr. Sam hat again and get into some chemicals that make a difference in your body. Because truly, your body is a remarkable system. It's constantly working to keep you synergistic, adapting to changes, and protecting you. But the thing is, your body doesn't know the difference between a real threat and a perceived one. It just responds. That's where cortisol, your body's stress hormone, comes in. Naturally, cortisol surges during specific times—when you exercise, wake up, or adjust to a new day. It's a part of your body's normal rhythm. But when you're in a constant state of stress, those levels don't reduce as well as they should. They stay high, keeping you on edge, ready for "fight or flight." And over time, this takes a toll on your body.

When cortisol remains elevated for too long, it doesn't just disappear. It finds places in your body to settle—often in your muscles or organs—waiting for the right conditions to resurface. This can lead to things like excess glucose production, weight gain, or inflammation. And here's the thing I tell my patients all the time: "Emotions aren't just in your head; they're in your body too. If you don't process them, they'll find somewhere to land." Your body is always trying to tell you something, and stored emotions are one of the ways it speaks.[3]

> Emotions aren't just in your head; they're in your body too. If you don't process them, they'll find somewhere to land.

Have you ever noticed how tension shows up in specific parts of your body? Maybe it's a headache that won't go away, tightness in your shoulders, or an ache in your lower back. For me, it's always the hips. That's where I store my stress, my sadness, my anger—all the emotions I try to push down when life gets overwhelming. I see the same thing in my patients. The chest, shoulders, back, and hips are common areas where the body holds onto unresolved feelings. And it doesn't stop there. Stored emotions can also show up as hormone imbalances, digestive issues, or even heart problems. That's because your body isn't just a collection of parts—it's an interconnected system. When one part is out of harmony, it affects everything else.

There's a growing understanding, even in Western medicine, that our emotions are energy. They don't just disappear when we ignore them. They transform and settle into physical symptoms, often in surprising ways. For those who study energy work, the connection between emotions and specific organs is particularly fascinating. In his book *The Emotion Code*, Dr. Bradley Nelson explains that emotions can originate in specific organs and lodge themselves anywhere in the body. For example, anger may start in the liver but find its way into your neck, your back, or your shoulders. Ancient healing traditions have long understood these connections, and modern science is starting to catch up. He further explains:

> Trapped emotions are always found to have emanated from a particular organ, no matter where that trapped emotion lodges in the body. For example, a trapped emotion of anger may have originally emanated from your liver, but it may come to rest anywhere in your body. It's important to realize that any emotion that becomes a trapped emotion may lodge literally anywhere in the body. Correlations between the organs and our emotions are both fascinating and important to our understanding of how our bodies really work. It all goes back to the ancient art of energy healing.

> For women especially, the hips and womb are often where emotions take root. This is why practices like yoga, stretch therapy, and energy work like Reiki frequently focus on these areas. Think about it: how often do we sit with our emotions, fully process them, and let them go? Most of us are too busy. We push our feelings aside, thinking we'll deal with them later—except later never comes. And so, those emotions stay with us, creating tension, pain, and other physical symptoms.

I've seen this in my own life. When I was pregnant with my second son, going through a divorce and holding on to so much anger, sadness, and guilt, I started experiencing debilitating hip pain. It wasn't just the physical strain of pregnancy; it was the weight of everything I hadn't let myself feel. My body was holding onto all the emotions I wasn't ready to face. It was a clear reminder that ignored emotions don't just vanish—they take up space in your body until you're ready to deal with them.

So, what can you do about it? How do you process and release those stored emotions so they don't wreak havoc on your body? The answer isn't a quick fix, but it's absolutely worth the effort. Start by slowing down. I tell my patients all the time, "You can't heal what you don't acknowledge." That means tuning in, paying attention to what your body is telling you, and creating space for your emotions.

Stretching and movement are incredibly powerful. Practices like yoga or targeted stretch work can help release tension, especially in areas like the hips. I often encourage my patients to pair movement with intentional breathing—slow, deep breaths that help calm the nervous system and signal to your body that it's safe to let go. Journaling can also be a helpful tool, giving you a way to put your feelings into words and process them in a structured way. And for those open to it, energy work like Reiki or guided meditations can be transformative.

You can't heal what you don't acknowledge.

The goal isn't to "fix" everything overnight. Healing is a process, and it takes time because it is a journey. But the more you listen to your body and allow yourself to feel what's there, the more you'll create space for balance and harmony. I always say, harmony isn't about erasing the hard stuff; it's about learning how to live with it, process it, and let it shape you in healthier ways. Your body wants to heal. All you have to do is give it the tools and the time it needs.

Understanding Your Triggers

One thing I always tell my patients is, "You can't manage what you don't understand." Triggers—those things that send you spiraling into stress, frustration, or even anger—are like signals from your body. They're telling you, loud and clear, that something isn't right. But too often, we react to the signal instead of figuring out what's causing it. The key is to understand your triggers so you can stop reacting and start responding.

First, let's get one thing straight: triggers don't just come out of nowhere. They're rooted in past experiences, unresolved emotions, or current stressors. Maybe it's the sound of someone raising their voice that sets you off because it reminds you of arguments you've heard in the past. Or maybe it's the feeling of being overworked and undervalued at your job that brings up old frustrations about not being appreciated. Whatever it is, your body is trying to protect you by sounding the alarm. The problem is, when you're constantly triggered, that alarm doesn't shut off. It keeps you in a heightened state of stress—your cortisol levels spike, your adrenaline kicks in, and your body thinks it's in danger, even when it's not.

So, what do you do about it? You start by identifying your triggers. This takes honesty, self-awareness, and a willingness to look at your life through a critical lens. Ask yourself, "What's happening around me when I feel stressed? Who or what am I reacting to?" Write it down if it helps. The more specific you can be, the better. For me, I've noticed that being rushed is a major trigger. It's something I've carried with me from childhood—always feeling like there wasn't enough time, always needing to move faster. When I'm rushing, I feel like I'm losing control, and that makes me reactive. But because I understand that about myself, I can now prepare for it and respond differently.

Once you've identified your triggers, the next step is to figure out what you can do about them. This is where the real work begins. If your work environment is a trigger, start by asking yourself what's in your control. For example, if you're overwhelmed by constant interruptions, can you set boundaries around your availability? Maybe that means not answering emails or text messages outside of work hours or before your day officially begins. I always tell my patients, "You teach people how to treat you." If you want your team to respect your time, you have to model that behavior yourself. Set clear expectations, communicate your boundaries, and stick to them.

You teach people how to treat you.

If your triggers are at home, the first thing to consider is whether your environment is safe. Let me say this loud and clear: if you're living in a situation where you feel threatened—physically, emotionally, or otherwise—it's not something you should handle alone. Reach out to a licensed therapist or the proper authorities for help. Safety is the foundation for everything else, and without it, your body will stay in survival mode, making it nearly impossible to find peace or balance.

But even in safe environments, home life can be full of triggers. If you're constantly dealing with stress at home, it's important to recognize that those triggers aren't likely to go away on their own. The hormonal toll of living in a high-stress state—where your cortisol is constantly surging—will wear you down over time. You may not be able to change the environment immediately, but you can start by changing how you interact with it. That might mean carving out moments of calm for yourself, whether it's taking a walk, practicing deep breathing, or finding a quiet corner to journal. Sometimes, it's as simple as creating small rituals to remind your body that it's okay to relax, even in the middle of chaos.

Harmony is about learning to live with the stressors while actively working toward the changes you need.

One of the biggest lessons I've learned in my own life is this: harmony isn't about eliminating all the things that stress you out. That's not realistic. Harmony is about learning to live with the stressors while actively working toward the changes you need. It's about finding small moments of stability and using them as stepping stones to bigger shifts. For example, when I was going through my divorce, my home became a source of constant triggers. Every conversation with my ex felt like walking into a minefield. I knew I couldn't change the situation overnight, but I also knew I couldn't live in that state forever. So, I started with what I could control: my reactions. Instead of letting my emotions run the show, I practiced pausing before responding. I gave myself permission to walk away when I needed to. And I leaned on my support system—friends, therapists, and even my journal—to process what I was feeling.

This isn't about perfection; it's about progress. You're not going to stop being triggered overnight, and that's okay. What matters is that you're paying attention, taking small steps, and giving yourself the grace to grow. Remember, your body isn't your enemy. It's always working to protect you, even when it feels like it's betraying you. The heightened feelings of stress, the racing heart, the tightness in your chest—those are all signs that your body is trying to get your attention. Listen to it.

Triggers are an invitation to learn more about yourself. They're an opportunity to understand what's happening beneath the surface and to create a plan for how to respond. Whether it's setting boundaries at work, seeking help for a difficult home situation, or finding ways to bring calm into your day, the goal is the same: to create a life where you feel more in control and less at the mercy of your stress. You don't have to get it right all the time, but every step you take brings you closer to the peace and balance you deserve.

Exploring Your Emotions

How you show up today isn't just about what happened in the last twenty-four hours. It's about everything that's ever happened to you. Every experience, every relationship, every joy, and every heartbreak—it's all still with you in some way. That doesn't mean you're trapped by your past, but it does mean that your reactions, your triggers, and even how you carry yourself are often shaped by things you might not even realize you're still holding on to.

This is why I tell my patients, "Your emotions don't just vanish. They linger, waiting for you to notice them." And when they pop up—seemingly out of nowhere—the goal isn't to run from them or blame yourself for feeling them. Instead, I encourage you to approach your emotions with curiosity. Be an observer, not a judge. This isn't about guilt or shame, and it's not about pointing fingers at who or what caused you to feel this way. It's about getting to the root of what's going on beneath the surface so you can begin to move through it.

Here are a few tools to help you explore your emotions in a way that fosters self-compassion, growth, and ultimately, harmony:

Questions to Ask Yourself

The first step in understanding your emotions is to start asking questions—real, intentional questions. When you notice yourself feeling off or having an emotional reaction that seems bigger than the moment calls for, pause and reflect. Ask yourself:

- *What happened in the last 48 hours?*
- *How about the last 24, 10, or even 2 hours?*

By working backward through these intervals, you can start to uncover what might have triggered your emotions. Was it a conversation you had? Something you saw or heard? Maybe even a moment you didn't think much of at the time? Give yourself the space to answer honestly without judgment. Curiosity is key here. The more you allow yourself to ask "why," the more patterns you'll start to notice. And those patterns can be incredibly telling.

For example, I've had moments where I'd feel this sudden wave of sadness and couldn't figure out why. But when I took the time to retrace my steps, I realized it was triggered by a comment someone made that reminded me of something my father used to say. It wasn't about the comment itself; it was about the connection it stirred in my subconscious. And once I understood that, I could start to work through it instead of letting it consume me.

Look for Patterns

Your emotions don't just show up randomly. There's a rhythm to them, even if it's hard to see at first. Maybe you always feel anxious at a certain time of day or in a specific place. Maybe you notice that you get defensive every time a particular topic comes up in conversation. These aren't coincidences—they're patterns. And once you start paying attention, you can begin to connect the dots.

When you identify these patterns, you give yourself the power to interrupt them. That's what I mean when I say, "You can't change what you're not aware of." Awareness is everything. Once you see the pattern, you can hit pause, take a breath, and decide how you want to respond instead of just reacting. It's like seeing the storm on the horizon and deciding to grab an umbrella instead of being caught off guard.

For example, if you notice you're always stressed at work around 2 p.m., ask yourself why. Is it because you're skipping lunch? Is it because you're dreading a certain meeting? Once you pinpoint the trigger, you can find ways to manage it—whether that's blocking off time to eat, rescheduling the meeting, or simply reminding yourself that it's okay to take a moment for yourself.

Ask Someone You Trust

Sometimes, we're too close to our own emotions to see the full picture. That's when it can be helpful to get an outside perspective from someone you trust. This isn't about giving someone else the power to define you; it's about asking for insight from someone who knows you well and wants the best for you.

When you ask for their feedback, listen. Really listen. Resist the urge to defend yourself or explain your actions. Just take in what they have to say. And whatever you do, don't use their observations as a reason to beat yourself up. This is about growth, not judgment. It takes courage to ask for help and even more courage to sit with the truth when someone mirrors it back to you.

I've had moments like this in my own life, where someone close to me gently pointed out a pattern I wasn't even aware of. It wasn't easy to hear, but it gave me the clarity I needed to start making changes. Remember, growth happens one step at a time. It's not about perfection—it's about progress.

Seek Professional Help

It's okay to need help. It doesn't make you weak—it makes you human.

Exploring your emotions can be a messy process, and that's okay. It's not supposed to be easy. But if you ever feel like it's too much—like you've opened a faucet only to find a waterfall—you don't have to go through it alone. This is where working with a professional can be life-changing. Therapists, counselors, or coaches who specialize in emotional regulation and trauma processing can help guide you through the heavy stuff in a way that feels safe and manageable.

I tell my patients all the time, "It's okay to need help. It doesn't make you weak—it makes you human." If you find yourself overwhelmed, reach out to someone who has the tools to support you. They can help you unpack your emotions, identify your triggers, and develop strategies to move forward.

Remember—You're Not Broken

Exploring your emotions isn't about fixing yourself because you're not broken. It's about understanding yourself more deeply so you can show up in the world in a way that feels authentic and empowered. You might uncover things you weren't expecting, and that's okay. Be

Be patient with yourself. Be curious. And above all, be kind.

patient with yourself. Be curious. And above all, be kind. Healing isn't linear, and growth doesn't happen overnight. But the more you lean into the process, the more harmony you'll create—not just in your emotions, but in your entire life.

Tools for Processing Your Emotions

When it comes to processing your emotions, one of the most important things to remember is that your emotional and physical health are deeply connected. I tell my patients all the time, "What you allow into your mind affects your body, and what you do with your body impacts your mind." That's why taking care of yourself requires a balance of mental, emotional, and physical tools. Here are some practical ways you can start making space for your emotions and supporting your overall well-being.

Limit Negative Mental Intake

There's a lot happening in the world that's out of your control. Whether it's the latest tragedy on the news or the fear-inducing stories in a true crime podcast, the content you consume matters. When you constantly take in negativity, your brain starts to believe that fear and danger are everywhere. I always say, "Your mind believes what you feed it." If you're constantly feeding it stories of harm and distrust, your body will respond with heightened stress, tension, and even avoidance of things that could bring you joy.

That doesn't mean you should live in a bubble and avoid all news or media, but it's about setting boundaries for your mental health. If you notice that you're feeling anxious or afraid, trace those emotions back to what you've been consuming. Did the fear start after binge-watching a crime documentary or scrolling through a particularly grim newsfeed? If so, consider limiting how much of that content you take in.

Instead, balance staying informed with staying present. For example, if you enjoy walking or running in the park but feel unsafe after something you've seen or heard, take steps to feel more secure. Put in one earbud instead of two so you can stay aware of your surroundings. Invite a friend to join you or look for a community walking group. The goal isn't to retreat from life; it's to find ways to engage with the world in a way that feels safe and empowering.

Cold Plunges

Cold plunges are one of my favorite ways to help the body reset. Spending just a few minutes in cold water challenges your body and mind in ways that are both uncomfortable and transformative. As your body reacts to the cold, your mind has to decide whether to stay or retreat. That tension between discomfort and resilience strengthens your mental fortitude. And the benefits don't stop there. Cold plunges reduce inflammation, promote weight loss, tone your body and skin, and even support better organ health.

I've had patients tell me that cold plunges feel like hitting a reset button—not just for their bodies, but for their emotions too. When you step out of that cold water, you feel a sense of accomplishment, strength, and clarity that carries into other areas of your life. It's a great way to remind yourself, "I can handle this," even when life feels overwhelming.

Hydrotherapy

If cold plunges sound a little too intense, hydrotherapy might be a great alternative. This involves alternating between hot and cold water, which helps to reduce inflammation and refocus your mind. The sensation of shifting temperatures draws your attention to the present moment, grounding you in what your body is experiencing instead of what your emotions are feeling.

Hydrotherapy can teach you patience. It's a way of reminding yourself that you can handle more than you think, one small step at a time. It's not just about the physical benefits—it's about training your mind to stay present and resilient in the face of discomfort.

Hydration

It might sound simple, but hydration is one of the easiest and most powerful tools for improving your emotional and physical health. When your body is hydrated, your cells can function at their best, which means your energy levels, mood, and overall well-being improve. I always tell my patients, "Water is life. Treat it like the gift it is."

But staying hydrated isn't just about drinking more water; it's about nourishing your body with healthy fluids that support detoxification and cellular health. You can enhance your hydration by adding things like lemon, chia seeds, or berries to your water. These small additions not only improve the taste but also provide your body with antioxidants and nutrients that make hydration even more effective.

Your Sleep Cycle

Sleep is one of the most underrated tools for emotional processing. It's your body's way of renewing itself, but you have to actually sleep for that to happen. If you're struggling to maintain a healthy sleep cycle, it's time to take a closer look at what might be getting in the way. Ask yourself:

- ¤ What's my physical environment like? Is it too warm, too cold, or too noisy?

- ¤ How can I process my thoughts before bed so they don't keep me awake?

- ¤ When's the best time for me to put my phone away?

Your sleep environment matters just as much as your habits. Small changes—like creating a calming bedtime routine, using a fan for white noise, or journaling before bed—can make a big difference. Sleep isn't a luxury; it's a necessity. When your body is rested, you're better equipped to handle emotional challenges with clarity and grace.

Releasing Emotions

Have you ever decided to declutter a room in your home? You know how it goes—it's a series of choices, big and small, that all come together to create a fresh, lighter space. You get to decide what stays, what gets donated, what gets sold, and what simply has to go. Maybe there's that little knick-knack you bought three years ago that you absolutely loved at the time. But now, it just sits there collecting dust, taking up space that could be used for something that makes more sense for the person you are today. Releasing emotions works the same way.

Letting go of an emotion isn't about denying that it existed or pretending it wasn't important. It's about recognizing that the story and the response that came with that emotion no longer serve you. You get to look at that old emotional reaction, acknowledge it for what it taught you, and say, "You know what? You're not who I am anymore. You've gotta go." It's a choice—an empowering one—that allows you to make space for new emotions and healthier responses that honor who you are now.

But here's the thing: all emotions are signals. They're your body's way of getting your attention, asking you to address something deeper. When you work to release older, stored emotions, it doesn't mean you'll never feel that way again. Emotions will always come and go—it's part of being human. What changes, though, is your ability to process and move through those feelings without letting them take over. The more you practice releasing old emotions, the easier it becomes to handle new ones when they show up.

Releasing emotions is about lightening your emotional load, one piece at a time. It's about making room for the feelings you want to cultivate in your life—joy, peace, resilience—and learning how to navigate the ups and downs with grace. And just like decluttering, it's a process that gets easier the more you do it.

Journal Reflection: Clearing Space for New Emotions

Grab your journal, find a quiet space, and take a few moments to explore these prompts. Let yourself be honest and open—you're creating a safe space to process and release what no longer serves you.

1. Recognizing Emotional Reactions

- What are some emotional reactions you've noticed in yourself that no longer feel helpful or aligned with who you are today?

- What triggers those reactions? Be as specific as possible.

- How do you typically feel after reacting that way? Does it leave you feeling drained, angry, or unsettled?

2. The Power of Letting Go

- What positive outcomes could come from letting go of those old emotional responses?

- If you could replace those reactions with something new, what would that look like? How would it feel?

3. Slowing Down to Release

- What's your favorite way to slow down so you can safely release old emotions? Is it through deep breathing, journaling, meditation, movement, or something else?

- How does your body feel when you take the time to release stored emotions?

4. Welcoming New Emotions

- Once you've let go of old emotional patterns, what are some emotions you'd like to experience more often in your life? Write them down and describe how they feel.

- Why do these new emotions feel more aligned with the person you are today?

- How can you reinforce these emotions when old triggers start to resurface?

5. Tuning In to Positivity
- What are some of your favorite ways to tune in to your more positive emotions? Maybe it's through spending time in nature, connecting with loved ones, or engaging in a creative activity.

- How can you make space in your daily life to experience these emotions more consistently?

Remember, releasing emotions isn't about perfection—it's about progress. It's about learning to listen to what your body and mind are telling you and giving yourself the grace to move forward, one step at a time. Just like clearing out that cluttered room, it's a process that takes time and intention. But the result is worth it—a lighter, freer, more aligned version of yourself, ready to embrace the emotions and experiences that truly serve you.

Moving Forward

Taking care of your emotional health starts with listening to your body and using tools like these to support it. But remember, it's not about doing everything perfectly—it's about finding what works for you and committing to small, consistent steps. Whether you're setting boundaries with the media you consume, stepping into cold water for a few minutes, or simply drinking an extra glass of water each day, every little action adds up.

Now that you've got a foundation for processing your emotions, it's time to turn your focus to your physical health. In the next chapter, we'll dive into the importance of movement and flexibility in creating a life that feels balanced, strong, and vibrant. Because when you take care of both your emotional and physical health, you set yourself up for the kind of harmony that supports every area of your life.

Chapter 6

CARE FOR YOUR PHYSICAL WELL-BEING

Remember in college I joined a Sunday morning walking club through my church? At the time, I was just beginning to experience the benefits of consistent chiropractic care after years of migraines, fatigue, and tension that seemed impossible to shake. And that walking club met at a park where we'd walk a mile and a half loop together before sharing a meal. What struck me most was how

Movement became more than just exercise; it became a source of freedom, vitality, and connection.

everything began to shift: I had more energy, better focus, and deeper relationships with the people I walked with. Movement became more than just exercise; it became a source of freedom, vitality, and connection. To this day, I credit those walks for teaching me how movement and harmony in the body go hand in hand. It's not just about moving for the sake of moving—it's about moving in a way that aligns with who you are and how you want to feel.

Hearing that you should take care of your physical health isn't groundbreaking news. We've all heard it, right? For me, this has been a lifelong journey—a mix of trials, lessons, and triumphs—but one thing I know for sure is that it's a journey worth taking. When most people think about physical health, the first thing that comes to mind is exercise. And while movement is important, let me tell you—there's so much more to the story.

Two pieces of the puzzle that don't get enough love are flexibility and mobility. These are foundational to your health and well-being, and if you ignore them, it won't matter how many steps you take or how much weight you lift—your body will eventually let you know it's not happy. Not sure how? We're going to break it all down with my Dr. Sam hat on for this chapter.

Discomfort and pain are signals, not a life sentence.

Flexibility is your muscles' range of motion—how far they can stretch comfortably without resistance. Mobility, on the other hand, is about how well your joints move. It's the teamwork between your joints, muscles, tendons, ligaments, and the overall health of those components that determines how fluidly and intentionally you can move. For your joints to do what they're supposed to, all those pieces have to be working together, like an orchestra.

Every part—your muscles, joints, tendons, ligaments—has its own instrument to play. When one of those instruments is out of tune, the entire symphony suffers. That's why flexibility and mobility are so important. They allow your body to move in harmony, without pain or restriction, so you can fully engage in your life.

Let me ask you something: have you ever looked at someone and thought, "They look healthy," or the opposite, "They must be unhealthy?" It's okay, we've all done it. But here's the truth: health isn't something you can see just by looking at someone. The World

Health Organization defines health as "a state of complete physical, mental, and social well-being, and not merely the absence of disease or infirmity."[4] Think about that for a second. *Complete* well-being—not just "I feel fine."

The reality is, most people who walk into my practice and claim they're healthy are actually out of alignment with that definition. Take stiffness, for example. If you're twenty-five and you're waking up stiff, that's not normal. And if you're forty-five and thinking, "This is just part of getting older," I'm here to tell you that's not true either. Stiffness—whether mild or severe—is your body's way of sending you a message. It's saying, "Hey, something's off, and I need you to pay attention." Discomfort and pain are signals, not a life sentence.

And here's the good news: there's no better time than right now to listen to what your body is telling you. Start moving in a way that supports long-term health instead of brushing those signals aside.

When you stretch, you're not just helping your muscles loosen up—you're giving them the opportunity to grow, adapt, and elongate. Stretching is about creating space in your body for movement, energy, and healing. Unfortunately, the opposite is also true. When you don't stretch, your muscles can become tight, develop adhesions, and lose their ability to function properly. This limits your range of motion and sets you up for injury.

I've seen it time and time again with patients who spent years bodybuilding without paying attention to flexibility. They loved how they looked in the mirror, but their bodies told a different story. Over time, their muscles became so tight that their joints were practically stuck. They ended up with limited range of motion, chronic pain, and a reduced quality of life.

Here's how I explain it: ignoring flexibility is like driving a car with misaligned tires. Sure, the car will still move, but it's only a matter of time before something breaks down. Your body works the same way. Without the natural elongation that stretching provides, your body compensates in ways that aren't sustainable.

Let's get one thing straight: moving your body isn't about chasing perfection or punishing yourself for what you can't do. It's about honoring what you *can* do and building from there. Whether it's walking around your neighborhood, spending five minutes stretching in the morning, or practicing yoga, the goal is the same: to create harmony within your body.

When you prioritize movement, you're not just improving your physical health. You're giving your mind and emotions the space to thrive. You're creating alignment in your body and mind that supports your overall well-being. That's why flexibility and mobility matter. They aren't "nice to have" extras—they're essential parts of living a vibrant, pain-free life.

So, as we dive deeper into the importance of flexibility, mobility, and movement, I want you to pause and reflect. Ask yourself: *What's one small way I can create more space for my body to move freely? What type of movement feels good for me right now—not just for my body, but for my overall sense of well-being?*

Start there. No pressure, no perfection—just intentional movement that honors the person you are today. Let's explore this together.

The Science on Sedentary Lifestyles

It's been years since *Time Magazine* published their article comparing sitting to smoking, and let me tell you—it made waves. I remember referencing it constantly with my clients back then, using it as a starting point to talk about just how damaging prolonged sitting can be to the body. The research they cited painted a clear picture: sitting for long periods of time is linked to heart disease, diabetes, obesity, and hypertension. For years, we thought this was because people who sat more were less likely to exercise. But the reality is, even if you're hitting the gym regularly, prolonged sitting has a way of undoing the benefits.

Here's the thing: there's a big difference between sitting too much and not exercising enough, and they both affect your body in unique ways. Standing and moving throughout the day changes how your body uses energy, how it burns calories, how it stores fat, and even how your brain processes information. The *Time* article highlighted a fascinating statistic—high school students who stood during class instead of sitting improved their test scores by 20%.[5] That's the power of movement.

But here's where things get even more sobering. A review of forty-three studies analyzing daily activity and cancer rates found that people who spent more hours sitting had:

- A 24% greater risk of developing colon cancer
- A 32% higher risk of endometrial cancer
- A 21% higher risk of lung cancer

And this was *regardless* of how much they exercised. Let that sink in. Even if you're working out regularly, the hours you spend sitting can still put your health at risk. Another study found that for men and women who exercised the same amount, each additional hour of sitting was associated with a decline in fitness levels. In other words, sitting has a way of quietly chipping away at the benefits of the work you're doing to stay active.

I say this to my patients all the time: "Your body was designed for movement." It's not just about the hour you spend at the gym—it's about how you use your body throughout the day. When you're moving, even if it's just walking around the house or doing light chores, your body is actively using energy to keep your cells functioning properly. This is where something called Non-Exercise Activity Thermogenesis comes into play: it is all the energy you burn through daily activities that aren't formal exercise—things like standing, walking, cleaning, or even fidgeting.

Your body was designed for movement.

But when you sit for extended periods, your body's natural processes start to slow down. The signals that prompt movement become less active, while the processes that encourage fat accumulation become more dominant. It's like your body gets stuck in a holding pattern, making it harder and harder to get up and move. Over time, this not only affects your physical health but disrupts the harmony between your mind, body, and emotions.

Why Aren't We Moving?

Modern life has us stuck in a cycle of sitting and stressing. Most of us spend the majority of our day sitting—at work, in the car, on public transportation—and it doesn't stop there. You leave work mentally drained from all the tasks, deadlines, and responsibilities, and by the time you get home, your energy is tapped. You've still got dinner to make, kids' appointments to keep, or errands to handle, and the last thing you want to do is get up and move. Your body craves rest, but your brain won't stop running through tomorrow's to-do list.

And let's be honest, unresolved emotions don't help. As we talked about in Chapter Five, avoiding those feelings often looks like numbing out in front of the TV with your favorite drink, trying to decompress. On top of that, financial stress might make you hesitant to invest in a fitness app or gym membership. It's easy for movement to slide all the way to the bottom of your priority list.

But here's what I hear from clients all the time: *"I'm tired of feeling stiff, sore, and uncomfortable in my body."* If that's you, you're not alone. The problem is, it can feel like a vicious cycle. You want to move, so you try something new, but the soreness afterward discourages you from continuing. That frustration leads you back to doing nothing, which makes you feel even worse, and the cycle repeats.

I hear a lot of reasons people avoid movement. Here are the ones that come up the most:

¤   "I just don't want to."

- "There's not enough time in my day."
- "I can't stick to a consistent routine."
- "It hurts, and that scares me."

And every time, my response is the same: "Your well-being is worth it." Start where you are and don't overthink the "how" just yet. We'll get to that. The most important thing is to begin.

Here's something that might surprise you: the more you move, the more energy you have. And the less you move, the less energy you'll feel. If you're feeling sluggish and unmotivated, one of the best things you can do is push past that initial fatigue and move your body. You'll be amazed at how much better you feel afterward.

Your well-being is worth it.

Movement isn't just about getting stronger or burning calories. It's about helping your body function the way it's meant to. When you exercise, blood flows through your joints, carrying away toxins that can cause stiffness and inflammation. Over time, this increased circulation can improve flexibility, reduce pain, and support healthier joints.

Even something as simple as drinking more water makes a difference. Hydration helps your cells expand and thrive, flushing out toxins that restrict your range of motion. It's a small step with a big impact.

I love saying this: *motion is lotion*. When you move your body, you're essentially lubricating your joints, reducing tension, and calming irritation. Movement doesn't just make your body stronger—it makes it happier.

So if you've been avoiding movement because it feels overwhelming, I want to encourage you to start small. Stretch for five minutes in the morning. Take a short

Motion is lotion.

walk around your block. Dance in your living room. It doesn't have to be complicated or perfect—it just has to be intentional. The key is to get moving, even if it's just a little bit, and let your body feel the benefits of motion.

A Flexible Body Creates a Flexible Mind

Flexibility isn't just about whether you can touch your toes or pull off a perfect split—it's so much deeper than that. I believe that when you cultivate flexibility in your body, you create space for a more flexible mind as well. The two go hand in hand, and when you take a holistic approach to flexibility, integrating both the physical and mental aspects, it can transform your overall well-being.

One of my favorite things about movement is how it creates space for inspiration.

When you move your body—whether it's through stretching, yoga, or just flowing with intention—you're not just increasing your range of motion or protecting yourself from injuries. You're unlocking something bigger. Stretching and moving release endorphins, your body's natural "feel-good" chemicals, which help reduce pain, boost pleasure, and create an overall sense of well-being. That's why movement is such a powerful tool for managing stress and improving mental health—it literally helps you feel better from the inside out.

When your body is free of tension, your mind follows. It's like a ripple effect—when you feel physically great, your creativity, focus, and clarity improve too. You start noticing new possibilities, solving problems more easily, and embracing an abundant mindset. That's the beauty of it: as your physical body opens up, so does your mental capacity to see the world in new and exciting ways.

One of my favorite things about movement is how it creates space for inspiration. Have you ever been in the middle of a workout and suddenly had an incredible idea pop into your head? That's no coincidence. Being in motion helps your brain process and connect ideas in ways it can't when you're stuck sitting still. And here's the best part: while you're moving your body, you can also be feeding your mind. Listening to a motivational podcast, taking in a series you love, or even soaking up positive input from a great audiobook can amplify those feel-good vibes.

If you're someone who can walk on a treadmill and read a book at the same time, I applaud you—that takes some serious skill! But whether you're multitasking or simply enjoying the movement itself, the point is that you're creating an experience where your body and mind are working in harmony.

Recently, I came across something Corey Muscara, a mindfulness coach I follow, shared: "What if purpose is just a moment-to-moment conversation with your soul? What brings me alive in this moment of my life? Versus, what is my purpose in life?" I love this because it speaks to the idea that purpose—and flexibility—can evolve over time. Just like a muscle that needs regular stretching to stay strong and pliable, our minds need to stay open and adaptable to grow.

When we stop stretching—whether it's physically or mentally—things shrink. A muscle that isn't stretched begins to tighten, the fibers mat together, and eventually, it can cause pain. It's the same with your mindset. A closed mind keeps you from trying new things, from putting yourself out there, because you're afraid it might be uncomfortable or even painful. But the truth is, staying stagnant hurts more in the long run.

Just like a muscle that needs regular stretching to stay strong and pliable, our minds need to stay open and adaptable to grow.

Immobilization limits not just your body but your ability to think clearly.

Think about this: how often have you sat at your desk, stuck on a problem, telling yourself you won't move until you figure it out? The longer you sit, the more frustrated you get, and the solution feels further away than ever. That's because immobilization limits not just your body but your ability to think clearly.

Movement, even something as simple as stepping away for a walk, unlocks your ability to problem-solve.

Mobility and flexibility are more than just physical perks—they're the foundation of a healthy, functional body. When you work on these areas, you're not just preventing injuries or improving your performance during physical activities; you're also enhancing your posture, balance, and even how you feel mentally and emotionally. It's all connected, and as I always say, "Harmony in the body creates harmony in the mind." So, let me leave you with some simple, effective ways to enhance your flexibility and mobility right from the comfort of your home.

Lacrosse Balls / Foam Rolling

I'm not going to sugarcoat it—soft tissue release isn't always pleasant, but using a lacrosse ball or foam roller is one of the best tools for breaking up adhesions in your muscles and increasing joint mobility. Think of it as giving your muscles the TLC they need to move freely again. To use a foam roller, apply it to the muscle you want to target and roll from one point of insertion to the other. Focus on areas like your back and legs—two of the most common places where tension likes to hang out. For the smaller areas like under your feet, or between the shoulders, you can squat against a wall with a lacrosse ball and go to town feeling the amazing release that can give you. Please avoid rolling the ball or using the roller directly against your spine.

Pectoral and Door Stretches

With how much time we all spend sitting, pectoral stretches are like a reset button for your upper body. They help relieve stiffness in your chest, trapezius, and shoulders, which can all become tight from hunching over desks, phones, or computers.

Exercise Bands

I'm a huge fan of band pull-aparts for opening up your chest and strengthening your back. They're simple, but don't let that fool you—they're incredibly effective. Grab a resistance band and pull it apart while keeping your shoulders down and your movements controlled. These are great for anyone who wants to combat that hunched-over posture we all seem to develop after hours at a desk.

Seated Stretches

If you've got an office job, seated stretches are your new best friend. These aren't just for the first thing in the morning—you can set a timer throughout your workday for quick ten-minute breaks to work on your flexibility and wake up your body.

Forearm Releases

For those of you who spend hours writing, typing, and clicking a mouse, forearm stretches can be a lifesaver. Carpal tunnel is a common issue, but daily wrist mobility exercises can help prevent it. Try this: lace your fingers together and gently push your wrists back and forth toward your forearms. Then, hold your fingers with your opposite hand and press them gently toward your inner forearm. Finally, hold your hand parallel to the floor and use the other hand to press your fingers side to side. Another helpful tool could be to use a massage gun with a focused attachment on the forearms (inner and outer), from the muscle insertion points at the elbow towards those at the wrist. Your wrists and forearms will thank you!

Ergonomic Workspace and Posture

Let's talk about your workspace. I tell my patients all the time, "Your posture is your power." If you work from home, take a minute to check your setup. Snap some pictures or record yourself sitting as you normally would (don't cheat by trying to sit perfectly for the camera!). Then, compare what you see to ergonomic recommendations you can easily find online. Small adjustments can make a big difference. If you can, invest in an ergonomic chair that supports your back and encourages proper posture.

Sit-and-Stand Desk

If you have access to a sit-and-stand desk, use it! But here's the trick: alternate between sitting and standing throughout the day to avoid putting too much strain on your body while in either position. When standing, use an anti-fatigue mat under your feet to reduce pressure on

A body in motion stays in motion, and that's where the magic happens.

your legs and back. And don't forget to wear supportive shoes while you're at it—your body will feel so much better by the end of the day.

These simple tools and strategies are here to help you feel better, move more freely, and create a body that supports your goals—not holds you back. As I always say, "A body in motion stays in motion, and that's where the magic happens." Let's take it one stretch, one roll, and one small adjustment at a time. You've got this!

Simply Start

When it comes to creating a movement routine that sticks, start small, and keep it simple.

Let me make this simple: when it comes to creating a movement routine that sticks, start small, and keep it simple. You don't have to climb a mountain on your first try—just put one foot in front of the other. The key is to find something that resonates with who you are and where you're at right now. If you pick something too intense or overwhelming, it's going to be tough to stick with it—and then you'll feel frustrated, and we don't want that.

Here's the thing: movement doesn't have to feel like a chore. One of my favorite ways to enhance a workout is by pairing it with music. And we're not just talking about having fun—there's science behind it! Music interacts with your brain's neural circuits for movement, which is why it can elevate your mood, distract you from fatigue, and even increase your endurance. Songs with a good rhythm can help you keep a steady pace, making exercise feel easier and, dare I say, even fun. For example, research shows that cyclists who pedal to the beat of their favorite music actually use 7% less oxygen.[6] That means their bodies are working more efficiently just because of rhythmic cues from the music. How cool is that?

So, ask yourself: *What sounds like a fun way to move my body?* Maybe it's Zumba, yoga, barre, pilates, or cardio dance. When thinking about it gets you excited to jump in, you're more likely to stay consistent and actually enjoy the process.

If joining a gym or paying for a fitness class doesn't feel right for you, don't worry. There are so many free resources out there—apps, YouTube videos, and online workout plans from personal trainers that allow you to get moving in the comfort of your own home. If you feel like spending money on a fitness app will hold you accountable, go for it! And if the idea of swapping your streaming service subscription for one that supports your health sounds appealing, that's an easy switch. Just think: instead of binge-watching a show, you could be binge-building a healthier version of yourself.

For those of you who want to get out of the house, you've got options too. A gym near your workplace can make it easy to work out during lunch or on your way home. If you're an early riser, many gyms open early so you can get your movement in before your day starts. There's a reason so many high achievers swear by working out in the morning—it jumpstarts

It doesn't have to be complicated—it just has to happen.

your energy and sets the tone for a productive, positive day. It's like coffee, but better!

And don't underestimate the power of a simple walk—like my walking group all those years ago. Throw on some sneakers and head to a park, stroll through your neighborhood, or take a walk during your lunch break. If you're a mom managing a busy household, put your little one in the stroller and meet up with a "fit mom" group for a walk. Sometimes, moving with others can keep you accountable and make things more enjoyable. Look for community groups that meet for hiking, beginner yoga, or other activities. Knowing you've committed to moving with others not only motivates you but gives you something to look forward to.

These small acts of movement can keep your joints happy, your tension low, and your body moving freely. It doesn't have to be complicated—it just has to happen. Here are a few tips to help you stay consistent:

- Pick a time: Choose a time of day that works best for you and commit to moving every day.

- Talk to your chiropractor: They can help guide you toward movement options that fit your health needs.

- Try it for three weeks: Stick with one thing for three weeks before switching it up or adding something new.

- Stay flexible: If you get bored with one routine, try another. Just don't stop moving.

- Ask yourself these questions: *Would I rather move solo or in a group? Do I want to work out at home or in public? Would an app, a gym membership, or a personal trainer help me remain motivated?*

The answer is yours, and there's no wrong choice. What matters is that you start. Remember, the path to a healthier you begins with one simple step.

Harmony in Motion

Movement isn't just about calories burned or muscles strengthened—it's about creating harmony within your body. When you move, you're supporting your circulation, enhancing your energy, and even regulating your emotions. Your body and mind are designed to work together, and movement is one of the best ways to bring them into alignment. Sitting for long periods interrupts that harmony. It's like leaving your car idling all day instead of driving it—it's not doing what it's meant to do. And the longer you stay idle, the harder it is to get moving again.

The big takeaway from all this is simple but profound: your body is made to move. Prolonged sitting disrupts how your body naturally uses energy, impacts your mental clarity, and diminishes your

Your body is made to move.

physical well-being. Moving requires intention, and let's be honest, it's easier to stay put than to make a change. But here's the thing: once you start incorporating even small moments of movement into your day, you'll notice the difference almost immediately.

It's not about overhauling your entire lifestyle overnight. It's about making intentional choices that honor your body's need for motion. Can you stand up and stretch every hour? Can you take a quick walk during your lunch break? Can you swap the elevator for the stairs? These small actions add up, and they create the kind of harmony that keeps your body, mind, and spirit working together instead of against each other.

Movement isn't a chore—it's a gift.

Movement isn't a chore—it's a gift. It's how you reconnect with yourself, how you honor the incredible instrument that carries you through life. So as we dive deeper into why movement matters, I want you to ask yourself: *What's one small way I can honor my body's need for movement today?*

Now, let's continue to self-reflect as you work on how to channel positive energy in Chapter Seven.

Chapter 7

CHANNEL POSITIVE ENERGY

After my divorce, I knew I had to start doing the real work—the kind of work that forces you to sit with yourself, take a hard look at where you've been, and decide where you want to go next. It wasn't a linear process. Let me tell you, healing rarely is. But step by step, conversation by conversation, I began to chip away at the pain, the anger, and the self-doubt that had been sitting under the surface for far too long.

Therapy became a safe space for me to process and release some pretty intense emotions. Week after week, I'd show up and unpack the things I hadn't even realized I was carrying. One thing I learned during this time was the importance of investing in yourself—mentally, emotionally, and physically. If you want to grow, you have to give yourself the tools and the time to make it happen. Shifting mental health is no different from the physical health within the body. It is consistency with doing the work necessary that is required.

If you want to grow, you have to give yourself the tools and the time to make it happen.

As part of my healing journey, I joined a mindfulness group for leaders led by a friend, Sky Jarrett. She held retreats in Jamaica, a place that has always held deep significance for me and my childhood

105

growing up there. My first retreat was life-changing; I learned how to truly slow down, to breathe, to sit with my thoughts without judgment. It was like peeling back the layers of who I thought I was and reconnecting with the person I wanted to be, really getting in tune throughout my body and soul. That retreat set something in motion for me—a reminder that harmony isn't something you stumble upon; it's something you create.

Harmony isn't something you stumble upon; it's something you create.

By the time my second retreat came around, I felt like a different person. I posted a picture on social media of myself getting ready for the trip, a big smile on my face, radiating excitement and gratitude for the opportunity to go back to that space of renewal. My caption was simple, something about looking forward to what the retreat had in store for me. But that post, really for me, represented so much more than just a trip. It was a reflection of all the inner work I had been doing—proof that I was stepping into a brighter, more intentional, more in tune version of myself.

Now, one of my former clients, someone I stay connected with on social media, commented on that post. We've always kept in touch, liking and commenting on each other's stories and posts, but her words that day stood out. She wrote, "I don't know what you've been doing, but keep it up! You're glowing, and I love to see it!"

Her comment hit me in a way I didn't expect. It was like she held up a mirror to my face and said, *"All that work you've been doing? It's paying off."* That glow she mentioned wasn't just about the smile on my face—it was the light that comes from within when you start to heal, when you start to align with who you are and what you're meant to be. Living and healing in harmony is about allowing life to unfold,

It was the light that comes from within when you start to heal, when you start to align with who you are and what you're meant to be.

being present for it, and like the waves on the cover illustrate . . . being like water, with all its movements and forms.

The truth is, healing and growth radiate outward. When you take care of your mind, body, and spirit, it shows in how you move through the world. You start to attract the kind of energy you've been cultivating within yourself. That's what that comment reminded me of—that when you do the work to invest in yourself, it doesn't just stay inside. It shines through, in ways you can't always see but others certainly notice.

> *The more you pour into yourself, the more you create space for joy, light, and possibility.*

I realized at that moment that the glow my former client was seeing wasn't just about where I'd been—*it was about where I was headed*. And that's the thing about healing: it's not a destination; it's a journey. The more you pour into yourself, the more you create space for joy, light, and possibility. And just like my second retreat in Jamaica, every new chapter brings with it a chance to grow even deeper into the person you're meant to be.

Here's the thing, it can take someone else's words to remind you how far you've come. And for me, her comment was that reminder—that all the work, all the tears, all the moments of sitting with my discomfort were worth it. *I was living in alignment with*

> *I finally realized that life was happening for me, not to me.*

my values, radiating positivity, and creating a life filled with purpose and peace. That's what I call harmony, and it's the kind of work I'll always be committed to.

You may think life stopped happening to you then. That it just all became butterflies, rainbows, and nothing can touch you. Actually, it's the opposite.

I finally realized that life was happening for me, not to me.

I finally accepted that some days are lived by the minutes and the milliseconds of breaths needed to get me through it all. I realized that if it will be, it is up to me to decide. In this very moment, as

I write, life is beautifully happening: children playing then crying, planning for attendance at a concert in a few hours, deadlines looming as well as playing catch-up on what has already happened. The task list is exceptionally lengthy as I manage my anxiety around all of that is unfolding for me.

I could fill you in on more details of disappointments that have led to major dilemmas, decisions of the unhealed past catching up to me tenfold, and the unfolding of big decisions ahead of me that are equally overwhelming and disappointing while very much exciting. Living in harmony dictates that we take life as it comes, we plan for the unexpected amidst the achievement of our goals, and find joy in the journey—with all of the emotions in tow. We surround ourselves with tools that will enable us to shift us into our true selves daily, knowing that life is connected and you are never truly alone.

It is worth it to figure yourself out and invest in yourself, especially when you feel that pull that you are ready for the next best phase of growth in your life.

Furthermore, let me explain it like this: when you are doing this kind of work for yourself, it opens your heart and frees your mind. You show up differently, because who you are and your ways of being are so much more authentic that you can't help but attract even more positivity from the world around you. You have more joy, more energy, and more light. Those feelings create a greater purpose for you.

It is worth it to figure yourself out and invest in yourself, *especially* when you feel that pull that you are ready for the next best phase of growth in your life. Personal growth is an ever-evolving process. When you get to one level, the next one is on its way, but only when you are open to it. That is what I recognized as I went through the same personal growth material the second time with my new perspective. The way I see it—I wasn't starting from the very beginning, I was just going through it with new eyes, learning even more about the way past events shaped me, and understanding that I can decide which lessons still make sense for me and which no longer fit the person I'm becoming.

In all of that personal self-reflection, one memory of my father kept coming back to me. I remember him telling me as a child, "Don't leave the table unless you've finished your food." It seemed simple enough at the time—a lesson about not wasting food, about appreciating what you have. But as I've unpacked it over the years, I've come to realize how deeply it shaped the way I thought about the world.

You see, I didn't just hear it as "*Finish your meal.*" Not to his fault, what I internalized was the belief that if I didn't take everything in front of me *right now*, it might not be there when I needed it later. That one idea planted a seed of scarcity in my mind—a feeling that opportunities were limited, that if I didn't grab them the moment they appeared, they'd be gone forever. The way I saw it was like I was constantly racing against an invisible clock, saying "yes" to everything because I was so afraid of missing out.

And let me tell you, this scarcity mentality showed up in so many areas of my life—work, relationships, especially my health. I felt like I had to do it all, take every chance, and push myself to the edge just to make sure I didn't miss an opportunity. But here's the thing: living that way isn't sustainable. It's exhausting. And it's based on a lie. Opportunities aren't like that plate of food on the table— they don't just disappear if you don't devour them immediately.

It took years—and a lot of inner work—for me to reframe that belief. I had to remind myself, *"There's enough for everyone, including me."* Opportunities don't vanish the moment you let one pass by. In fact, sometimes the best thing you can do is step back and ask, "Does this really align with who I am and where I want to go?"

It's about knowing when to say yes and when to let go.

Because not every opportunity is meant for you, and chasing them all will leave you running on empty. What is meant for you will never miss you.

The truth is, my father's lesson, while well-intentioned, left me with a mindset

I've had to unlearn. But in doing so, I've realized that abundance isn't about taking everything you're given—it's about trusting that there will always be more when you need it. It's about knowing when to say yes and when to let go. And let me tell you, that kind of shift doesn't just create space in your schedule—it creates harmony in your life. And that's what I'm always striving for: balance, alignment, and the trust that everything meant for me will come in its own time.

At an abundance and prosperity workshop with Chris Lee, I learned more about how to shift my mindset from scarcity and lack into one of abundance. I realized that there are opportunities out there for all of us, and no one was going to rob me of mine. It's important to pursue them with health rather than agreeing to everything and running myself into the ground out of fear that if I didn't pursue them right away, they'd go away and never return.

It's true that the way we think directs the way we feel about life in general. When you feel good, life seems a bit sunnier. On days when you aren't feeling so great, you automatically want to feel coddled and cozy under your covers because it feels physically comforting. It doesn't necessarily foster a positive attitude, but it may give you the space to feel your feelings, take a nap, and feel better when you wake up.

"Watch your thoughts; for they become words. Watch your words; for they become actions. Watch your actions; for they become habits. Watch your habits; for they become character. Watch your character for it will become your destiny." I've seen this quote from Lao Tzu show up in my reality again and again. It's important to remember that *you get to choose how you want to show up.* The day isn't shot because you wake up in a mood. In this instant, shift it. It's your decision, make a different one.

You get to choose how you want to show up.

Make it Okay to Play

Most recently, I've been studying emotional intelligence, learning how to look at my past and the different situations that influenced my mindset. I've learned how to shift those experiences into a more powerful way of being as I continue to reconnect with my true self. And let me tell you, I've learned that it's okay for me to have whatever feelings I have. I can express myself in a way that is helpful to everyone involved, and I can decide when pausing and thinking before responding makes more sense. My ability to deeply listen and stay present instead of listening to react has also strengthened over the course of my learning.

I've spent so much time working on my inner child, and the most beautiful part of that work has been rediscovering that she's still there, alive and well, just waiting for me, adult me, to nurture her. The magic of this personal growth journey is how much my two boys reflect my inner child back to me. Every single day, I see glimpses of her in them—the way they laugh, dance, and sing with abandon, the way they approach the world with curiosity and wonder. Especially my youngest. Not only does he look just like me at his age, but his energy is so pure, so joyful—it's like looking into a mirror of who I was and who I still am deep down.

And that's the key I've found: my children are my daily reminder of what truly matters. They pull me out of my *"go, go, go"* mode and remind me to pause, breathe, and reconnect with joy. My boys invite me—no, they insist—that I step into the world of play with them, and I've realized just how much I need that. They've become my greatest teachers, showing me the power of being present, of finding lightness in the small moments, and of allowing myself to just be. In fact, I've read more children's books, played with more dinosaurs, and walked around outside today than I planned.

> *Because what I've learned is this: joy is a healer.*

And you know what? Playing with them is such a healing space for me. It doesn't have to be a grand production or some carefully planned event. My boys have taught me that joy is in the little things. It's dancing around the living room like nobody's watching, making up silly songs while we clean up their toys, or even just running through the yard chasing each other like we're playing tag for the first time. Every time I engage with them in this way, it's like I'm telling my inner child, *"Hey, I see you, and I'm here for you."* Because what I've learned is this: joy is a healer.

When I look at my boys, I see they're growing up so fast, and I know these moments won't last forever. But what they've taught me about play—that it's not just for kids, that it's necessary for all of us—will stay with me for the rest of my life. Because when I let myself play, when I step into their world, I'm learning to live with more joy every day.

Dare to Stop Comparing

You've heard that comparison is the thief of joy, I'm sure, and I agree. Think about the impact social media has on your life. Do you ever just scroll on your phone aimlessly? Let me tell you, scrolling gives you a plethora of opportunities to easily compare yourself and your entire way of being to anyone who shares a post.

Here's the thing: when you look at a picture on social media, you don't know if that is the twentieth version of the same shot unless they choose to let you in on the secret. Far too many of the posts you see are a small fraction of a person's life being highlighted. They are picking and choosing what parts of their life they want to share. I loved it when my friend commented on my picture the day I was feeling incredible and looking forward to my next retreat. She wasn't comparing my life to hers, but rather encouraging me to keep moving forward. She was creating harmony, like two instruments in sync—each playing its part, complementing the other, and making something even more beautiful together. It wasn't about overpowering or competing; it was about finding a common tone, and letting both of us be heard.

There is a difference between comparing yourself to someone else and allowing yourself to learn from them. It's okay to hear someone's story, learn from the lessons they've learned, and apply what you learn to your own life rather than thinking you wish you could be who they are. At the end of the day, you only know as much about someone's life as they choose to tell you.

If I'm being honest, I found myself comparing my business outcomes to someone else's, and it made me feel like what I was doing wasn't enough. Even though my business was thriving, comparing it to someone who experienced a different level of success diminished all of the hard work my team and I put into where we were at the time. And you

> *There is a difference between comparing yourself to someone else and allowing yourself to learn from them.*

know what? I later realized that the other business owner may have made more money at the time, but they were also struggling with problems that I had, and those that I didn't have.

When you feel your mind wandering into comparison, take a moment to focus on where you are now and how far you have come instead. It could be a span of a decade, a year, a month, or even a day. The truth is, where you are today is perfect, and due to the fluidity of life, it won't remain the same tomorrow either.

Your Brain Finds What You Choose to Seek

Let me tell you something incredible—your brain is always working for you, even when you don't realize it. What you focus on grows— and that's not just a feel-good mantra—it's rooted in science. Your brain is wired to validate your thoughts and help you see the world in a way that aligns with what you believe. It all comes down to a part of your brain called the Reticular Activating System, or RAS.[8]

I'm going to put my Dr. Sam hat back on and let's figure this out together.

What you focus on grows.

The RAS is like the gatekeeper for your mind. It's a bundle of nerves at your brainstem that filters through billions of pieces of information around you and decides what to bring into your conscious awareness. Think of it as your brain's personal assistant, constantly asking, *"What's important to you? Let me find more of that."* It's why you can hear your name in a noisy room or suddenly start noticing a specific breed of dog everywhere after you've been thinking about getting one. It's not magic—it's your brain doing what it does best: focusing on what you tell it to look for.

Here's the thing—your RAS doesn't just work with random pieces of information. It's deeply tied to your beliefs and emotions. If you wake up and tell yourself, *"The world is full of kind and happy people,"* your RAS will filter your experiences to highlight every friendly smile, every positive conversation, and every small moment of joy throughout your day. You'll feel lighter, more open, and in harmony with the world around you. But if you tell yourself, *"People are rude and disconnected,"* your RAS will go to work proving that, too. Suddenly, you'll notice the person who cut you off in traffic, the stranger who didn't hold the door, and the coworker who seemed grumpy. It's all there in the same world—you just notice what you're focusing on.

Think of it like this: your RAS is why two people can have completely different outcomes in the same situation. Let's say two coworkers are given the same project. The person with a positive mindset thinks, *"I don't know all the answers yet, but I'm excited to figure it out."* Their RAS helps them see creative solutions, hear valuable input from others, and notice opportunities to learn and grow. Meanwhile, the person with a negative mindset might think, *"This is going to fail, and I don't even know why they gave it to me."* Their RAS focuses on what could go wrong, amplifies their doubts, and reinforces their belief that failure is inevitable. When things don't go perfectly, they're quick to say, *"See? I knew this wouldn't work."* It's not just about attitude—it's about how your brain is trained to process reality.

This is why it's so important to be intentional about what you focus on. The RAS is ready and waiting for you to tell it what matters, so why not point it toward the positive? When you set your intentions toward growth, gratitude, and opportunity, your brain will help you find more of it. You can literally train your RAS to work in your favor by visualizing yourself as a positive, capable person and reinforcing that image with action. It's not about faking it—it's about aligning your subconscious and conscious mind to create a new reality for yourself.

So, the next time you catch yourself focusing on what's wrong or what might go wrong, take a moment to pause and redirect. Ask yourself, *"What do I want to see more of? How do I want to feel?"* The truth is, your brain is always listening, and what you tell it will shape the world you see. That's not just science—it's the power *you hold* every single day.

> *When you set your intentions toward growth, gratitude, and opportunity, your brain will help you find more of it.*

Energy and Your Relationships

When you are working on yourself and trying to create a more positive outlook on life, it can be easy to think that you need to judge the people around you as positive or negative, and then you may feel an urge to let go of different relationships as you try to seek out like-minded individuals. My advice? For the moments when you begin to wonder about other people, slow down, take a deep breath, and look at yourself first.

Let's pause for a second and think about the people in your life, because I'll be honest, some relationships are easier to change than others. Take a good look at your job. If you don't like what you're doing or who you're doing it with, you can update your resumé and apply elsewhere. But (as I've learned firsthand) it can be more complicated with a marriage or a significant other. If you leave a relationship and begin a new one without getting curious about your role in why things didn't work, you may end up watching history repeat itself.

In my case, I didn't realize just how consistently it was showing up in all parts of my life during my divorce. I thought I was "*keeping home at home.*" But in reality I was bringing it all with me into our practice. My clients didn't know that, but my team knew something was going on based on the way I showed up. Well, I think my clients didn't know . . . however we are all connected, so it's possible.

Before I started my journey of self-development and shifting my ways of being, my team used to say, "We don't know which Dr. Sam is coming through the doors today." At the time, I thought I was doing a great job of keeping it all together, of hiding the chaos and frustration bubbling just beneath the surface. But I wasn't. Not even close.

What I didn't realize then was that even though my team didn't know the specifics of what I was going through, my tone, my temper, and the way I responded to things spoke volumes. My words said one thing, but my energy told the truth. I was unpredictable and reactive because I was carrying so much I hadn't dealt with, and they felt it—even when I thought I was hiding it well. It was as if the tension inside me walked into the room before I did, and that weight began to push them away.

Eventually, my team started to disassociate from me. And I don't blame them—I wasn't showing up for them in the way they needed. Looking back, I see how my inability to manage my own emotions created distance and they were just protecting themselves from the energy I didn't even know I was putting out. That was a hard truth to face, but it was also the wake-up call I needed to start doing the real work. Because the way I was showing up wasn't just affecting them—it was a reflection of how deeply disconnected I was from myself.

What I've learned is this: when you start to seek harmony and you begin to shift the way you are, how you think, and what you want in your life, you begin to formalize a clear vision about what matters to you. When you make changes, the new version of yourself reinforces and strengthens how you show up. As your experiences shift, you may find yourself shifting away from others who you may not have much in common with anymore or whose energy doesn't align with yours.

If you want to find like-minded people, you have to start by fully understanding what is in your mind. You can just as easily find a negative or a positive like-minded person. You can attract and reinforce your ways of being in either direction based on who you choose to look for. The more comfortable you become with the person you want to be, the easier it is to attract the right people into your life. It just takes practice and presence.

The more comfortable you become with the person you want to be, the easier it is to attract the right people into your life.

Your Presence is a Powerful Gift

Let me tell you something: oftentimes, people can feel like they're walking around feeling unseen. Being present helps you to see who someone is and connect with their humanity. Sometimes the best thing you can do for someone is to just give them a hug. There is a difference between asking, "How are you doing?" and, "How are you *really* doing?" Responses to those two questions will vary based on the simple addition of one word. They go from, "I'm fine" to a much more open and vulnerable space when the person being asked understands that you are listening to what they are saying and that you are there for them at that moment.

Let me give you an example. One day at my practice, I personally adjusted forty-five people. In comparison, we had a total of forty-five people who came through the door for services with me *plus* the rest of my team one day earlier. Although adjusting so many people in one day could have been overwhelming and draining, I was truly happy to get to the end of that day knowing that from my first client to my forty-fifth, each one got the same level of care from me.

And real talk? The only way I could do this was with my support system. Rather than feeling like I needed to rush through my day, I asked my mom to pick up the boys and allowed myself to slow down. Because in those situations that

Being present is an invitation to be real with others.

require your presence, you have to make the commitment and be present. Those are the moments when you allow yourself and others to connect as human beings and share a positive energetic exchange. Being fully present gives you the opportunity to benefit from the experiences in your life instead of being in such a hurry that you miss having incredible conversations and interactions.

Being involved in personal development spaces, they always encourage us to look at each other and maintain eye contact. Looking at someone while feeling and really sensing the presence of someone who is standing there *with* you and *for* you can be very touching and bring forth some big emotions. That's the key.

What it comes down to is being present is an invitation to be real with others. Ten simple minutes of presence can feel like a lifetime for a person who really needs it.

Facing Life's Challenges

I have my faith in God that honestly helps me a ton when life doesn't go the way I would have liked. Because of my faith and the way it inspires me, I sincerely believe that everything will eventually work out the way it needs to.

The truth is, one of the best lessons I've learned is that everything is temporary. On the worst days of my life, there was a part of me that knew it wasn't going to last forever, and I could comfort myself with that knowledge. This is one of the reasons I love focusing on the natural world as it continues to show us that *nothing stays the same*—there is always sunshine after the rain, nighttime has a new day right behind it. Even when you lose a loved one, the intensity of the pain has a way of lessening over time. For me, I had to learn this the hard way with my dad's passing.

Growing up in Jamaica, my father was my constant. When my mom moved to the United States to pursue a better future for our family, he stayed behind and became the anchor for me and my siblings. He wasn't just "Dad"—he was everything. He worked as an accountant for one of the old sugar plantations, but that wasn't all he did. He ran little side businesses, kept the house running, and somehow managed to juggle it all while raising us.

When he wasn't working—which, I'll be honest, was rare—he was teaching us the value of responsibility and resilience. There were rules, structure, and expectations, but there was also this quiet love that you didn't have to question. He showed it in the way he provided for us, the way he kept everything steady while Mom was away.

I lost my dad on Memorial Day weekend, almost twenty years ago. I think about him every single year on that national holiday. And let me tell you, it still hurts, but it doesn't bite quite as much now.

I'm not going to sugarcoat it: some days are by the breath, the minute, or the hour. But, over time, I've learned the importance of letting myself process my pain rather than holding it in and then watching it pour out of me in horrible ways. I allow myself the time to breathe

> *Everything can get better, but the key is, it may just take time.*

more often, ask myself more curious questions, and work on creating thoughtful solutions around the different problems as they arise. No matter the duration of the challenge, my faithful perspective is that everything can get better. I'll say it again: *Everything can get better,* but the key is, it may just take time.

Trust me on this one, I can't overstate the importance of breathwork in your daily life. It isn't surprising that when you come out of a massage session or a restorative yoga class, a meditation or prayer time that you feel better. Breathwork slows you down. It can also help you ground yourself and focus more heavily on the present moment.

When I recently found myself having a challenging day, I tried focusing on my breath as much as I could. But you know what? There came a point when I just couldn't hold my tears back any longer, and I cried. I cried a lot. And that was okay. I'm human and I needed that release. When I went back to working with my clients, I did my best to provide the best service possible for them. Because I have worked with them and formed relationships, many of them gave back to me in some way that day—with a hug, an offer to pray with me, or a friendly squeeze of my hand, or even acknowledging the ways I have helped them. I received all of those little gestures and felt so blessed to have those people in my life.

Your life wasn't meant to be lived alone; it was meant to be shared in harmony with others.

Here's the thing—it's okay to stay open and be vulnerable with the right people when you need a little help with your bad days. I know, I get it. I like to keep up a mask of success and perfection too. But the only way to truly achieve harmony was by letting my people know how I was feeling that day; it gave them the opportunity to be there for me the same way that I show up and support them when they need me. In my moments of heartache and hardship, I had phone calls with my mom, a few trusted friends, my siblings, and my partner. They checked on me throughout the day by sending encouraging words, prayers, scriptures, quotes, and even a meme or two.

Your life wasn't meant to be lived alone; it was meant to be shared in harmony with others. Community is where we find balance— where the weight of the hard times becomes lighter because we allow others to carry it with us. The truth is, it takes courage to let people into both the good and the messy parts of your life, but when you do, you create space for connection, support, and growth. Harmony happens when we let ourselves be seen, and in those moments, the people who truly care for us will always show up.

Shifting Your Energy

Here's the thing, your energy levels are within your control, and some days are easier than others. Before I put in the work, I thought I was good at pretending things were fine when they were anything but that. I know better now. Sometimes, you need a little help to recognize your energy being sub par and then you can take steps to bring it up. Let's look at how you can get curious about your energy levels, and what you can do to make a positive shift.

Allow Others to Speak Into Your Life

One of the best ways for you to understand it's time to shift your energy is by allowing people you trust to check in with honest feedback. Rather than having an emotional reaction to them, thank them for their help, accept their feedback, and get curious when they point it out. Remind yourself that if these people ask if you are okay or suggest that you seem a little off, it's important to consider where your energy level is at and why. If you can't quite agree with the feedback, it's important to let it roll off of you, and allow time to settle it.

Analyze Your Daily Activities

You know, comfort food is a real thing. It may be gummy bears, alcohol, or an entire pint of ice cream. Set aside a few pages in a notebook to track your behaviors for three days in a row. Look for patterns with what you consume—foods, streaming services, social media, music, podcasts—all of it, and see if you notice any patterns.

The truth is you know yourself well enough to know when your energy is low based on what it produces as fruit in your life. For me? I know when my mind feels cluttered, my energy needs a shift. Allow yourself to be open to what you notice, and then choose to take action to make a change. Try the following tools when your energy needs a positive boost:

1. Listen to upbeat music and have a dance party.
2. Exercise.
3. Spend some time in nature.
4. Ground yourself.
5. Journal and get those feelings out of you and onto paper.
6. Talk to someone else.
7. Notice the origin of a pattern, then choose to interrupt it without blaming others.
8. Get a healthy amount of rest.
9. Sit outside and feel the warmth of the sun on your skin to create some Vitamin D.

Trust me on this one: it's easier than you may think to create a schedule that puts taking care of yourself as a top priority. If you're like me and you have a schedule that revolves around a service you provide for others or your kids and family, then there are pieces of your daily timeline that are already spoken for. So, when you can't shift your timeline, find places where you can fit time for you around that timeline.

I love to do things before bed. It helps me with an established sleep routine, and it's super simple. I turn off all of my electronic devices, allow myself ten minutes of mindfulness, stretching, and praying right before bed. And let me tell you, it's a beautiful ten minutes I get to honor myself and make sure my body is in tune.

If you are starting a new routine for yourself, choose ten minutes during a time in your day that makes the most sense for you. Those ten minutes can be sitting in your car during lunch, after you wake up and before you get ready for the day, or right before bed, like me.

Living with more positive energy in your life can attract more abundance, as you now know. Let's dive into our next C, which is all about celebrating and embracing the abundance in your life.

Chapter 8

CELEBRATE LIFE'S ABUNDANCE

I've heard that the right person can help you heal. With my heart so full of love and appreciation for the man in my life, I'm living proof—it's the truth. What I've learned is that in our relationship, we've been able to help each other continue to grow just by showing up as ourselves.

If you asked me several years ago if I could imagine being in a relationship with healthy boundaries and strong communication, I'd have said no. But here I am. Neither of us had to change into "the right person" for the other. We're just the right person for one another.

The beautiful thing is that when I met him, he hadn't gone through the self-development work I've done—the retreats, the emotional intelligence training—it's just who he was. One thing that attracted me to him was his openness and desire for growth. Trust me on this one, I can't wait to see what else he gets out of the workshops he plans to attend and how much more amazing he'll be because his ways of being have only gotten better from the ones he has attended. I love who he is. I know he's the person I've prayed, planned, asked, and even cried for. Having him in my life challenges me to continue to grow into the best version of myself.

If I'm being honest, most days in my relationship feel like we're still in our honeymoon phase. Don't get me wrong, we've had moments when there's some irritation. But those kinds of conversations when we work through a difference of opinion sound just like the way we talk to each other about anything else. They're boring—there are no raised voices or dramatic arguments. The mutual respect and love we have for each other doesn't change, even during challenging moments. You might not believe me, but some of those conversations have made our relationship even sweeter.

Because of who I am and who he is, we've found that we can just be ourselves. I can say, "When this happened, I felt this way," and he responds in kind with how he felt and the way he saw the situation. We thank each other for sharing a different perspective and move forward from there. It's incredible to be able to share our vulnerabilities in a safe space and find simple solutions to conflict.

When we met, he was very open about telling me that the number one thing he wanted out of our relationship was mature, healthy communication between two adults. We each had our own healing to do—both having children from previous marriages and going through divorces before we met. The openness, honesty, and vulnerability we share helps us continue to heal and grow closer to each other.

A lot of people are seeking a healthy relationship with a partner. But it has to start with looking in the mirror and figuring out where you are and what *you* need to do to be the person who attracts the kind of relationship you truly deserve. If enough people are telling you the same thing about how you're showing up, maybe it's time to pause for a second and dig into that. This process requires you to be less judgmental and more open to feedback. And please—let go of self-judgment. Instead of beating yourself up over past choices, it's better to choose from this moment forward to start doing better.

When you commit to going on a healing journey, you'll find that the work you do isn't just for your physical and emotional health—it also helps you become a different kind of partner within your relationships. And that's the key.

Shifting From Lack to Abundance

Most of us have been taught to spot the negative before the positive. Think about it: you could get almost every question right on a test, but your eyes go straight to the one you missed. We're wired to focus on what's lacking instead of celebrating what's going well.

Look at the ads we see everyday. They're designed to make us feel like something's missing—that if we just buy that *one* thing, we'll finally feel complete. How many times have you thought about something you didn't have or couldn't do over what you *do* have and *can* do?

Instead of looking in the mirror and seeing how individually beautiful you are, you automatically begin picking yourself apart—skin color, blemishes, wrinkles, freckles, hair type—there are so many things you can look at and want to change. Most times, once you change things, you're still not happy. You just find the next thing you need to change.

Those feelings of lack you experience are never truly about the makeup you use or the clothes you wear. When it comes down to it, those external changes aren't what can bring you lasting happiness. It's more about your heart and your mindset.

Let me give you an example. Early in my relationship, I kept getting signs that he was the one. But I struggled to accept it at face value. My past relationships had me second-guessing everything. I found him after he had been on a popular dating app for two days. After four days, it was my last day on the app, and something about his profile nudged me to message him.

One of the app-curated questions for his profile was, "What makes a healthy home?" His response was: "I think the best feature of a healthy home is having you in it." It showed me that he valued presence in relationships. I listened to the video he recorded, and I felt magnetized to this sincere and authentic person. I couldn't help but reach out. He replied to my message the following day, and we started getting to know one another. Three weeks later, we were in a relationship. Just like that.

The truth is, if you don't heal, you'll drag past hurts into your new relationships. I almost sabotaged ours because I kept waiting for the other shoe to drop. For me, he was too good to be true. I started doubting everything about our relationship.

My friends had to step in after listening to my concerns, by saying, "Yes. *OR*, you can start to just accept that this is all real. He is real. Give him an opportunity to be who he is, unless or until he shows you something otherwise."

Years later, he still hasn't.

This all ties back to the concept of "garbage in, garbage out." What you feed your mind becomes your reality. *When you fixate on what could go wrong, you start acting like it's already happening.* With my relationship, I could hear it, plain as day, that we harmonized together. But I wasn't willing to accept it. That's classic self-sabotage.

Do you ever do this to yourself too? Stop a good thing from happening because you're focused on what could go wrong? If, instead, you focus on abundance—on the good that's already here—you start to attract more of it.

To truly shift to an abundance mindset, you have to believe you're worthy of good things just as you are. That's it. No conditions. Your voice matters, your wants matter, and you don't have to prove that to anyone.

Emotional intelligence plays a big part in this too. The concept isn't something that is common to a lot of people. I think it's smart to explore it when you have the opportunity, because you learn how it can impact the way you show up on a regular basis as the best version of yourself. It's not just about reacting less; it's about learning how and when to respond.

I used to be the person who'd get a hundred positive reviews about my practice and fixate on the one negative one. That one comment would ruin my whole day. I wouldn't see it as happening *for* me. I would let it make me a victim and view it as something that happened *to* me.

After doing the mindset work I can now pause and ask myself, "What's this here to teach me?" I can shrug my shoulders and let those kinds of things roll off my back by pausing and seeing how it can work *for* me instead.

Even as a business owner, I've had to learn to shift from scarcity to abundance. I used to stress when clients backed out, thinking it was the end of the world. But now, I handle it with grace. It's like if a musician misses one note, they don't just stop playing their masterpiece. They keep going.

Recently, a new client who'd prepaid for her care asked for a full refund after finding out what her insurance wouldn't cover even after much explanation. Instead of spiraling, I processed the refund right away and said, "Perfect. This is great. I'll take care of this for her."

My intern looked at me like I was crazy, but I told her, "This is a 'yes' moment for me."

Of course it is important to have the money coming in to pay my team and myself. But the people we get to work with matter even more than the bottom line for me. For this client, I couldn't wait

You see, energy is a choice.

for her to let go of the way her body responded to all the heavy things going on in her life, and help her to release those stored emotions.

By honoring that client and giving her what she needed in that moment, I knew it wasn't a time for feeling like she was the last person we'd ever meet. There would be more clients. The mindset shift that you can create is an instantaneous choice.

You see, energy is a choice.

When you choose an abundant mindset, you show up differently—more positively, more creatively, and more excited about life. That's why I ask my team every day, "What are you bringing to the shift? Who are you choosing to be?" And time and again, that energy attracts the right clients, heartfelt testimonials, and those beautiful moments of connection that make it all worth it.

When you build your life from the perspective of what is right with the world instead of what's wrong with it, you can see the cup as half full rather than half empty. I still remember the first time I heard that phrase, and I wondered, "What is the cup?"

I've learned that the cup is all the things you want it to represent—you, your mind, your way of thinking and seeing the world. The healing I went through was necessary to help me unlock the real me. It started with healing my inner child and some things I had honestly forgotten about over time.

As I remembered things while going through the emotional intelligence work, I was easily able to face old memories and work through those stored emotions.

When others shared difficult things they were going through, I could easily relate to their situations and offer my support as someone who had been there too.

I learned vulnerability is my superpower. Connecting to others and creating community is important and it often takes being open to your humanity and sharing it with others when appropriate.

The way I see it, when you build your life from a place of abundance, you start to see the world as half full instead of half empty. That's the shift—from lack to abundance. And it's *always* a choice.

GREET Positive Interactions

When was the last time you brushed off a compliment?

Why does it feel so much easier to dismiss it or explain it away?

If I'm being honest, one of the hardest things to do is simply to *receive*. It's right up there with trying to think positively. That all goes back to our negative programming—the way we fixate on our flaws instead of embracing what's good about us. Deep down, you might appreciate the compliment, but if you can't let it in, it never gets the chance to really lift you up.

I get it because I've been there. As a teenager, I struggled with feeling worthy of compliments. I still remember the comments people made about my acne and how small they made me feel. I could handle being called "cute" or having "a cute smile," but "beautiful" felt like a whole other level—one I wasn't sure I could ever reach. I spent a lot of time avoiding mirrors because I didn't want to get a close view of my face and the scarring on my acne-prone skin. I became used to looking directly at my hands as I washed them instead of looking in the mirror.

Back in high school, a friend once complimented my hair. Right away, I did what so many of us do—I started deflecting, giving all the credit to one of our other friends who had styled it. But she stopped me mid-sentence and said, "Sam, all you have to say is thank you." That moment stuck with me.

She handed me a metaphorical flower that day, and it's still blooming in my memory all these years later. It's a reminder of how powerful it can be to give people their flowers while they're here—to show gratitude for them in the moment.

When someone offers you a kind word, a helping hand, or a compliment, I want you to try this: GREET it. That means to *Graciously Receive and Embrace the Energy with Thankfulness.*

It really isn't as hard as it sounds.

Next time someone compliments you or offers to help, just pause, smile, and say, "Thank you." No explaining, no brushing it off—just a simple thank you. Yes, it might feel awkward at first, and your brain will try to jump in with a whole story to explain away the compliment.

Graciously Receive and Embrace the Energy with Thankfulness.

Let that go.

It doesn't matter what the compliment is—whether it's "You look amazing today," "You're so smart," or "You handled that like a pro"—*own it.* Let it soak in. Accepting positive feedback can genuinely change how you see yourself. When someone wants to help you, saying yes gives you a chance to build a deeper connection with them and allows them to feel good about what they're giving.

You are allowed to bask in those beautiful moments that pop up throughout your day. After all, it's who you are that attracts what you want most. Gratitude helps reinforce that. It shifts your focus to what's right in your world instead of what's wrong. The more you practice it, the more natural it feels to see the glass not just half-full, but sometimes even overflowing. And that's the kind of energy that can transform everything.

Tools for Celebrating Abundance

Gratitude reinforces who you are. It helps you stay present, positive, and connected to what really matters. When you start being thankful for the simple things—like food, a home, the people around you, or even just a beautiful day—you begin to see your own worthiness more clearly. *That kind of positivity doesn't just uplift you; it helps you create harmony in your life.* When you let gratitude lead, it's like tuning an instrument—you align yourself with a higher frequency, and that energy is contagious.

When you train your mind to focus on what's right instead of what's wrong, it's like finding the right notes in a song. Everything just flows better. You'll feel more creative, attract better opportunities, and stay grounded in the present moment. Gratitude helps you compose a life that resonates not just with you but with everyone around you.

So, if you're ready to shift into a mindset of abundance, here are some tools to help you fine-tune your harmony.

Download Your Day in a Journal

Journaling can do wonders for your mindset. Find a time that works for you—whether it's in the morning, during lunch, or right before bed—and list five things you're grateful for each day. Try this for three weeks straight and see what shifts. Pay attention to how your energy changes and how you start noticing more things to be grateful for. Remember, gratitude is contagious; you can even invite your friends and family to join in and share their five things too. There are apps in the App Store as well as gratitude-themed journals that could be available for purchase as well.

Look in the Mirror

This might feel a little awkward at first, but hear me out. It's time to start being your own best friend. Mel Robbins talks about the power of giving yourself a high-five in the mirror each morning. I get that it might seem silly but think about it this way: if a friend called you needing a pep talk, you wouldn't hesitate to lift her up. So why not do the same for yourself? When you look in the mirror, really look. Give yourself a smile, a high-five, or even a simple, "You've got this." You'd be surprised how powerful that little gesture can be.

Use "What if . . ." Statements

When life throws you into a mindset of lack, try flipping the script with "What if . . ." statements. Instead of spiraling into all the things that could go wrong, ask yourself questions that open up possibilities. For example, if you've lost a job, try asking, "What if this is actually making room for something so much better?" It's a small shift, but it creates a whole new energy—one that's rooted in abundance, not fear. This is how you create those "yes" moments that remind you that life is happening *for* you, not *to* you.

Embodiment Exercises

You've probably heard about saying "I Am . . ." statements. I like to take that a step further. Speaking affirmations is powerful, but *embodying* them takes things to a whole new level. Adding movement—whether it's dancing, yoga, or even a quick walk—helps your body absorb those positive words in a way that just saying them can't. There are affirmation soundtracks you can find online—some you can dance to, others you can stretch to. The point is to get your whole self involved.

Here are some of my favorite affirmations. Feel free to use any that resonate, or create your own:

- I am worthy.
- I am beautiful.
- I am strong enough for the moment I'm in right now.
- I am powerful with my words, and everyone wants to hear them.

Chapter 9

CREATE MEANINGFUL CONNECTIONS

Healing works best in community, but we've grown so used to doing everything on our own that we don't even realize the impact it has on us. The truth is, we've convinced ourselves that *lone-wolfing* it is somehow better, safer even. We avoid connection out of fear or limiting beliefs about how we can bring value to our relationships.

Take a moment and think honestly about how you interact with people. When was the last time you walked up to a stranger, looked them in the eyes, and just said, "Hello?" That one simple word can spark a conversation that leads to an authentic connection—something real between you and another human being. When was the last time you did something so simple yet so profound?

I always say that putting yourself out there takes courage, but that doesn't mean I've always followed through on my own advice. When I first heard about The Summit of Greatness, I knew I wanted to go. I knew Lewis Howes and his podcast attracted a certain type of person—people who want to grow, manifest greatness, and shift into new ways of being. But, truth be told, I didn't have the confidence to go alone. I was so worried about sitting alone, not having a friend to talk to, and *looking* lonely. So, I stayed home. I immediately regretted letting my fears hold me back from all that I could have received at such a powerful growth experience.

By 2023, though, I'd done enough healing to feel stronger in myself. I gathered the courage to attend The Summit of Greatness solo, and if I'm being honest, it was one of the best decisions I've ever made. I can see myself on stages soon, speaking at workshops, giving keynotes, even doing TED Talks. I want to leave a larger imprint on this world. I went to soak up all the motivation I could and to connect with incredible people. I reminded myself to stay open to whatever opportunities came my way—and to have fun.

As soon as I got in line for registration, I noticed a young woman from Bermuda. She had dreadlocks like mine and just radiated good energy. I said, "Hi," and she said, "Hi," with a big smile and warm energy, and that one little greeting turned into introductions to more and more people. Within twenty-four hours, I went from being alone to having a tribe of twelve. We hung out the entire weekend, and two weeks later, she visited me in Atlanta. All of that happened because I was willing to greet a stranger.

The beautiful thing about this is that connection doesn't have to be complicated. My youngest son is proof of that. He's a social little guy. He'll walk right up to another kid at the park and ask, "Want to play?" No hesitation, no second-guessing.

My older son, being autistic, has more moments when he doesn't want to be bothered. He is working on his sentence structure, and he's learned to tell me clear as day, "I don't want," when he would rather not play. It makes me wonder: Why can't we, as adults, do that? Why can't we say hello when we're curious about someone or be honest when we want or don't want something?

I used to hate group projects in school. I was always the one doing all the work, and it felt pointless to even have a group. I'd wonder why I couldn't just go somewhere by myself and do the whole thing without having to worry about the other people trying to pretend like they contributed in some way.

As adults, we say it's much harder to make friends than it was when we were kids. But when you think about it, our friendships weren't really born in the reality of life. Now that we have so many more options as adults than we did as kids, we make it more complicated than it needs to be.

In school, I began to learn that groups could be dangerous when you are with the wrong kind of people. Several times, I was on the receiving end of cruelty for no reason. I thought certain people were my friends, and they'd turn against me, and over time, the lone wolf in me grew much stronger than the pack wolf, and I began isolating myself. But even a lone wolf still needs to be among the pack at some point.

I remember being so annoyed as a child with the "it is what it is" conversations. My favorite word was, "Why?" It annoyed the heck out of my family. They'd ask me why they had to answer so many questions and my response was always the same. *I needed to know why.* It was just that simple for me.

That one word has made me the practitioner I am today. I love helping my clients understand why things are happening the way they are, and why they want to become a better, more aligned version of themselves. I love that my business comes from a place of educating and sharing information with clients at all times.

The way I see it, anything worth doing requires a strong why—especially healing. If your why isn't strong enough, it won't hold up when things get hard.

For me, my *why* is my children. I want to be the best mom I can be, to teach them how to be stronger and better than I was, and to support them through their own journeys. Because the truth is, if I can't face my own fears, how can I inspire them to do the same?

> *Anything worth doing requires a strong why— especially healing.*

Establish Healthy Boundaries

Creating boundaries in your life is one of the most loving actions you can take for *yourself*. It's a way of showing that you understand the importance of having moments when you need to just be "off." You need people around you who get that too: people who support healthy ways of thinking and living, and who aren't afraid to set their own boundaries either.

Boundaries help you create healthy guidelines for how you interact with the world. When you're able to discuss them openly, it gives everyone the clarity they need to avoid those awkward or draining situations later on. I always say that the more you can express why a boundary is important to you, the easier it is for others to respect it instead of trying to cross it.

To create a new boundary, start by recognizing that you are important—your thoughts, your actions, what you want out of life, and how you want to show up *all matter*. So, if you notice something happening that doesn't align with who you are or what you stand for, you have every right to let others know what you will no longer accept. Let me give you an example.

I know some friends who won't answer texts or phone calls between certain hours because that's their time to be present with their children. And you know what? I don't feel upset or offended by it at all. We've established boundaries to respect each other's personal space, and it makes our friendships stronger.

Personally, I have a firm boundary about being mindful of who I speak to and when. I used to feel like I had to be available all the time—no matter what. I'd leave conversations feeling completely drained because the person on the other end was just taking and taking. That's when I realized how unhealthy that was for me.

I used to lean hard into people-pleasing. I'd help folks without even thinking about it, only to realize later that they were never going to reciprocate. Watching them make decisions based only on what they needed opened my eyes to just how toxic my habit of people-pleasing had become.

A friend of mine had to set some boundaries at work. Her boss started calling her on her days off and late into the night, long after her workday was supposed to end. She let him know—respectfully but firmly—that she would only take calls during business hours.

And guess what? The world didn't end. Her boss adjusted, and she felt so much better for standing her ground.

For me, as a business owner, I've had to create boundaries that respect both my time and my team's. Sometimes everything feels urgent, but I pause and ask myself if it's really going to get better results at 9 p.m. or if it can wait until the morning when we're all back in the office. (You already know which option wins every time.)

You may have heard, "your vibe attracts your tribe." You get to decide how you engage with people. Not everything is for everyone, and that's perfectly okay. The way I see it, when you feel how you feel, there's always a reason for it. You're allowed to honor that, without judging yourself or worrying about what someone else might think.

Creating healthy boundaries is truly an act of self-love. They might not be popular with everyone involved, and that's okay. These kinds of choices aren't easy, but it all comes back to one simple question: Who are you honoring in this situation? Trust me on this one: *you're allowed to be at the top of your priority list.* For way too long, women have been told that we have to be self-sacrificial at all times. But what actually hurts when we do that? Everything and everyone else around us suffers when we aren't healthy minded or bodied. It's not worth the sacrifice; you matter! No one is touting that selfishness is the goal either. Set healthy boundaries knowing that is a demonstration of love to yourself, and ultimately to others.

> *Creating healthy boundaries is truly an act of self-love.*

Appreciate the Pack, Flaws and All

It took me a while to really recognize just how much of a lone wolf I am. One of my coaches once told me that some parts of who we are might never change completely—we just learn how to manage them differently. And honestly, I think that's true. It's not about getting rid of those parts of ourselves; it's about learning how to work with them so we can still show up, enjoy the journey, hit our goals, and create the kind of impact we want to leave behind.

The reality is if I want to create a bigger impact and build a legacy that's strong and healthy, I can't do it alone. I've realized that I have to step outside of myself sometimes and actually ask for help. Lone-wolfing it all the time doesn't feel good anyway. Sometimes, you need that accountability—whether it's from a group or even just one other person—to help you stay committed to what matters.

When I decided to write this book, I knew doing it alone wouldn't be nearly as powerful as creating it with my team. I've learned how to hone my ideas, dig into different research, and share my voice in a way that feels completely authentic to who I am. There are days when I look back at what we've created, and I just think, "Wow, that really came out of me? That's wild."

I've built up a lot of strength from doing things on my own for so long. I'm comfortable in that space. I won't lie and say I'll never go back to lone-wolfing again, because I still do in some ways. But I also know that if I want to grow, I have to create space and opportunities to join a community and lean into being more of a pack wolf. And that means accepting people as they are—flaws and all.

The beautiful thing about being part of a pack is that everyone has their imperfections, just like I do. People will disappoint you. They'll say things or do things that hurt. But when you're strong enough in who you are, those things don't cut as deep. The more I do the work to strengthen my sense of self, the easier it becomes to see my own worth. I can confidently say that I am a beautiful person. I do have value. My opinions matter, and the ideas I have to share with the world are important.

Confidence doesn't mean arrogance. You can be humble and still own what you bring to the table. If you're lone-wolfing it all the time, you might miss out on some incredible opportunities, whether that's finding the love of your life or building a community that supports you. If you go into every situation thinking that all people are selfish or that all men are jerks, that's exactly what you're going to find. I've chosen to look for evidence that challenges those negative beliefs, and I believe that choice has kept me on the right path.

I have been blessed to have a very supportive family, and a crew of friends curated over time. Without them, life would have been a little too hard, and for way too long. Sometimes, the community looks like just one person—my partner. Other times, it's a church group I visit to see if I want to be a part of it. Depending on the situation, a community could be a whole organization or just a small group within it.

Being part of a community requires an open mind and a willingness to embrace new opportunities. I remember attending a leadership academy where I was one of only three Black participants in a group of fifty. There were two Asian attendees, and the rest were White. I couldn't help but think about how much more powerful that experience would have been with more representation.

Imagine how much we could heal—culturally and personally—if more of us had access to those kinds of spaces. We all have unique experiences simply from the space of just how we are raised and the heritage we have—our family histories and how those experiences impacted our ancestors and our parents.

My parents were raised a certain way. Their way of thinking about and interacting with the world impacted how I grew up, what I was and wasn't exposed to, and the limiting beliefs and mindsets my upbringing created in me. Those real things can be more culturally appropriated than anything else. My reason for believing that everyone could benefit from attending a leadership academy is simple: the more we understand ourselves and each other, the easier it is to come together in more authentic ways.

Being part of a community requires faith in people. Not everyone has been through what you've been through, and they're going to bring different perspectives and experiences to the table. That's not a bad thing—it's part of the beauty of community. But it does take courage and a recognition of the human condition. No one is perfect. Not you, not me, not anyone.

I expect people to rub me the wrong way from time to time, and I'll most likely be that kind of person for someone else. I always say that if I don't show up for you perfectly every single time, I hope you'll give me the same grace I give you. Because there will come a day when we show up for each other in a beautiful way. That's just how it works. There is a level of acceptance necessary to be in community.

So, if you're tired of being hurt or drained by others, I get it. It's easy to want to close yourself off. But it's not fair to judge others for their low energy when we've all had those days. It isn't fair to expect others to show up in a way you can't be in that moment. I'll say it again: No one is perfect.

And that is okay.

The sooner we accept that, the easier it becomes to truly appreciate the pack, flaws and all.

Support Groups

Finding your like-minded tribe tends to happen organically as you move through your healing journey. Sometimes, that journey starts by going to a therapist who can recommend different kinds of support groups—whether online or right in your local area. Having a tribe that gets you can make all the difference.

Typically, support groups for people who have dealt with trauma are led by folks who have the training and experience to really help their attendees. The best way to find a solid support group is to seek the help of a professional first. That way, you won't end up in a space that's more triggering than healing. Trust me on this one— being mindful about the groups you choose can save you a lot of heartache.

Some of the things I did to help myself heal were originally out of reach for me financially. I remember looking at retreats and workshops and just thinking, "How am I ever going to afford this?"

But I consider myself blessed to attract goodness. I found retreats that offered discounts and ways to make it work. The beautiful thing about the healing journey is that when you're really committed, opportunities have a way of showing up.

That said, it's not just about money. There are some groups that just don't seem to fit where you are on your path—and that's okay. *It's more about finding a tribe that feels right for you, people you're comfortable being real with.* The way I see it, it's not about forcing connections; it's about finding your people, the ones who truly get it. Across the years, I have taken the time to cultivate my tribe. It's truly been a blessing to have such good friends in my circle.

If you're not sure where to start, here are some questions to ask yourself to find a good fit:

- Do I align with this group's mission and vision?
- Does this feel like a judgment-free space?
- Am I able to be open and honest in this group?
- Is there a list of agreements that the group follows, including confidentiality?
- Can I see myself learning from this group?
- Are the group members going to influence my growth in a positive way?
- Do I feel like joining this group will help me shift into a new way of being?
- Does this group resonate with me and my intentions?

Allow yourself to get curious about the kind of group you might like to join. But don't ignore your gut. If it doesn't feel like a safe space where you can work toward your goals and grow into a better version of yourself, then it might not be the right fit.

Your tribe is out there, I promise. It might take a little searching and a lot of discernment, but you'll find them. In the meantime, give yourself the grace to keep looking until you do. The right people will show up when you need them most.

Being Social

For all the lone wolves out there, the thought of joining groups and being social on a regular basis might feel completely overwhelming. It's easy to say you don't need anyone, but humans are wired for connection. We were created to be communal.

We were created to be communal.

Our need for socialization is why we're always looking for someone to bounce ideas from, someone to talk to, someone to share experiences with. The right kind of group can help you see when you need support—and can connect you to resources you might not have known about otherwise. So if you're ready to take a step out of your lone wolf ways, here are a few ideas to help you meet new people. Remember, putting yourself out there with an open mind can lead to all kinds of new opportunities.

Try a Combo

One way to meet new people is to combine something you already do with an organized group. It could be as simple as finding a group exercise class, signing up for a book club, or going to a local paint-and-sip. Once you've signed up, you can actually look forward to being involved in something you already enjoy. The beautiful thing about this is that it takes the pressure off because anyone you meet chose to be there too. So, you already have one thing in common.

Online Groups

If in-person meetups feel like too much right now, online groups can be a great way to ease into things. Meet-up and Facebook groups are filled with people who share your interests or life experiences.

Maybe you start with a mom group and discover that a few of the other moms love wineries or that they share another interest you're passionate about. Meeting up can feel way less awkward when you already know you have something in common.

List Your Interests

When was the last time you made a list of things you genuinely enjoy doing—or things you've been wanting to try? Sometimes just naming those ambitions that have been sitting on a shelf for "some other day" can reawaken a passion. Maybe you want to start gardening again or write a book. Once you've got your list, do a little research. Find a local event or a group that matches up with what you're interested in and see what shows up for you.

Find Me Online

There are all kinds of ways to keep the conversation going and connect with like-minded people who are ready to level up their lives. For those of you looking for encouragement, motivation, and practical tips to keep you moving forward, you can also join my community at www.drsammarch.com. This is a space for people who want to Rmoniz™ and embrace the 6 Cs of Harmony in a real, meaningful way.

I always say that the more you realize you're not alone in what you're feeling—in your body or your mind—the faster you can make lasting changes. That's what this community is all about. It's a safe space to share your healing journey, ask questions, and support other growth-minded people along the way.

If you want to learn more about Rmoniz™ and the 6 Cs, my individual/group coaching, seminars, and other events, head over to www.drsammarch.com. Your tribe is out there, I promise. It's just a matter of stepping outside of the lone wolf zone and being open to what comes next.

Chapter 10

CONCLUSION

Reading this book wasn't about reaching some final destination. It's more like tuning your instrument before the next song starts. So don't think of this as the end. Think of it as a shift—your next movement in the symphony. I bet the next time you pick these pages back up, it'll hit differently—because *you'll* be different. Growth changes your ears. And every time you revisit Rmoniz™: 6 Cs of Harmony, you'll notice something you didn't hear the first time.

Now, I'm not claiming to be the first to talk about these ideas—the concepts and principles I've shared are universal. But I live by them. And my goal is to offer you simple truths with real steps you could walk out in your daily life. And what I've learned is, when I focus inward and show up fully—mess and all—I get to be the version of me that actually helps people.

That's the version I want for you, too. Because if each of us could show up aligned and tuned into who we're meant to be? Whew. *The harmony we could create would change the world.*

Let's pause for a second and look back at what you've learned.

Cultivate a Growth Mindset

An empowered mind can change your life. The best part is you get to choose how you show up every moment of your life. When life is "life-ing," you may need to consciously take a moment to slow down and flip your mindset so you can respond with grace.

Connect with Your Emotions

Ignored emotions become stored emotions. Giving yourself the space to understand your triggers can help you learn more about yourself. There is no shame in seeking professional help to have the support you need to process and release those long-buried emotions.

Care for Your Physical Well-Being

Motion (or lack thereof) feeds your emotions. The more you allow yourself to move throughout the day, the more energy you'll have. The opposite is also true. By enhancing your flexibility and mobility, you also give yourself permission to see the world with a general openness, making space for new opportunities.

Channel Positive Energy

Your spirit shines through when you prioritize your positivity. Letting go of comparison and setting your Reticular Activating System on the good things in life help you strengthen your sense of presence and gratitude. Remember, you have the power to choose the kind of energy you want to share with the world.

Celebrate Life's Abundance

You are worthy of abundance. Accept the blessings and beautiful moments as they are. GREET (Graciously Receive and Embrace the Energy with Thankfulness) compliments and acts of kindness from others with a simple, "Thank you." One more time, you are worthy of all the good things in your life.

Create Meaningful Connections

We're all interconnected. Although there are times when "lone wolfing it" feels good, there are also times when the support of the pack is necessary. Creating healthy boundaries is one way to ensure that you feel heard and seen within your community. Everyone is on their own journey, and we can all use some support from time to time.

Now that you've worked through the 6 Cs of Harmony, allow yourself some time to check on where you are on the self-evaluation chart below. Once completed, check your numbers with where you began in Chapter Three.

With each of the following questions, rate your current state: 1=never/low, 2=sometimes/medium, 3=always/high.

Physical Health		Mental Health		Energetic Health	
Stretch practice	1 2 3	Feeling sad	1 2 3	Prayer/ Meditation	1 2 3
Sleep quality	1 2 3	Feeling joyful	1 2 3	Personal spirituality	1 2 3
Immune health	1 2 3	Motivation	1 2 3	Mindfulness practice	1 2 3
Caffeine consumption	1 2 3	Control over emotions	1 2 3	Positivity	1 2 3
My daily energy level	1 2 3	My daily outlook	1 2 3		

When you finally recognize that you've been moving through life from a fractured place—and you start doing the real work to heal—that's when the melody starts to shift. You start changing the tune, one note at a time. But let me be honest with you: just because you're working on yourself doesn't mean life's going to quiet down and hand you a front-row seat to peace. Wouldn't it be beautiful if life just paused and said, "You know what? Let me give this woman some room to breathe while she heals?" But life doesn't work like that. No. Life's going to keep playing. And sometimes, it'll throw in a dissonant chord just to see if you've really learned the harmony. It'll test you—not to break you, but to see if the healing is sinking in.

I recently had a client I've been working with for a while who came in ready to engage with her sleep schedule. She was feeling good about many aspects of her life, and felt the next way to level up was to ensure that she was doing her best to get the rest she deserved. Rather than tell her it was a good idea and move on, I encouraged her to think it through during a conversation. I asked her:

- What could you do differently this week to get better sleep?
- What will your sleep schedule need to look like?
- If you feel better going to bed and waking up early, what hours make sense for you?
- Take your phone out and create a plan based on your current calendar.

The truth is, if you're not putting it into practice, you're not moving anything. You can read all the books in the world, but if you just close the cover and jump to the next one without doing the work? Nothing shifts. No shade—I love a good audiobook. I'll have one playing while I drive, cook, fold laundry . . . all the things. But let me tell you something: when I start hearing something that hits deep—something that makes me pause—I know I need more than just background noise.

That's when I go buy the book. Because once it's in my hands, I can highlight what speaks to me, jot down my thoughts in the margins, and go back to what stirred something in me. I've learned I'm a hands-on, visual learner. That means I need to *interact* with the material if I want it to stick. It's in the writing, underlining, circling, and note-taking that it really starts to live in me. That's when the learning becomes transformation.

When you think about the 6 Cs of Harmony, where are you in your level of readiness? Take a look at the following reflection questions and choose Y if you are ready to commit and N if you aren't ready yet.

6 Cs of Harmony Readiness Self-Assessment

6 Cs of Harmony	Readiness Reflection	Response
Cultivate a Growth Mindset	Are you ready to make yourself a priority on your daily schedule?	Y N
Connect with Your Emotions	Are you ready to face the past and work towards understanding, forgiveness, and freedom?	Y N
Care for Your Physical Well-Being	Are you ready to implement daily movement as a part of your lifestyle?	Y N
Channel Positive Energy	Are you ready to choose positivity in a way that feels authentic to you?	Y N

Celebrate Life's Abundance	Are you ready to embrace the good things in your life without being afraid of losing them?	Y N
Create Meaningful Connections	Are you ready to find your tribe and set healthy boundaries as you go?	Y N

Looking at the Cs where you circled Y, go through the following questions and apply them to the one area you want to work on implementing first.

- ◘ What will you do differently this week to get started?
- ◘ What will it need to look like for you to keep moving forward?
- ◘ What time of day makes the most sense for your implementation of this one new thing?
- ◘ Take your phone out and add it to your calendar, starting today if at all possible.

My goal was never for you to close this book and say, "Whew! I've got it all figured out now. Life = handled." That's not real life. So if you took that self-assessment and you're sitting at a three thinking, *"I've still got a long way to go"*—that's okay. You're not behind. You're becoming. And this right here? This is why community matters so deeply. Because when you know you're still learning and growing, you start inviting in your people—your professionals, your people of peace, your friends, your family. You begin to see how every part of your circle plays a role in your harmony.

The beautiful thing about this journey is that it keeps unfolding. So let me leave you with this: keep going. Be gentle with yourself. Be gentle with others. You might be rockin' one part of your life right now, and that's worth celebrating. But life will always add new layers. And the more you surrender the stuff you can't control, and trust that all of it is aligning for your good—the stronger and more whole you'll become.

We're walking this out together. Still learning. Still tuning. Still growing—one C at a time.

Acknowledgements

To say thank you seems insufficient because the depth of lessons learned, and the abundance it will continue to provide is immeasurable. Nonetheless, I would be remiss if I didn't utter a few names.

Firstly, God—my business partner and life's fulfillment—without You, nothing would be possible. Second, my family (Cynthia, Miqui, Terry, Carl, Ryan, Jon, and Jordan) and my partner, Deej, have supported me through the darkest moments and shown me what support and community truly mean. Third, my dearest friends (Sherene, Twila, Marleny, Sky, Rain, Glen, and Susy), your support redefines friendship. Thank you for helping save my life. Fourth, my business world (Dr. J & the 100% Chiropractic family, Nicole Walters, and Relaxed Hustle), you've reminded me that life fulfillment is the goal, and it's up to me to redefine success. Thank you for the depth of your lessons! Lastly, my staff and dear patients in the Dunwoody, GA community—you're the real MVPs and have demonstrated for over a decade what the strength of commitment and community can create.

Thank you for your support and love.

Endnotes

Chapter Two

1. "5 Causes of Vertebral Subluxation: Unveiling the Hidden Culprits." HealthFirst Spine & Wellness, August 24, 2023. https://www.wellnessforaustin.com/5-vertebral-subluxation-causes/.

Chapter Three

2. Restrepo, Sandra, dir. *The Call to Courage.* Netflix, 2019. https://www.netflix.com/title/81010166.

Chapter Five

3. Nelson, Bradley. *The Emotion Code: How to Release Your Trapped Emotions for Abundant Health, Love, and Happiness.* New York: St. Martin's Essentials, 2019.

Chapter Six

4. "Constitution of the World Health Organization." World Health Organization. Accessed July 22, 2024. https://www.who.int/about/governance/constitution.
5. Park, Alice. "Sitting and Exercise: How Much Do You Need?" Time, September 2, 2014. https://time.com/sitting/.
6. Jabr, Ferris. "Let's Get Physical: The Psychology of Effective Workout Music." Scientific American, March 20, 2013. https://www.scientificamerican.com/article/psychology-workout-music/.

Chapter Seven

7. Tzu, Lao. "A Quote by Lao Tzu." Goodreads. Accessed July 22, 2024. https://www.goodreads.com/quotes/.
8. "Reticular Activating System: Reticular Activating System/ RAS / Functions of Reticular Formation." YouTube, March 6, 2021. https://www.youtube.com/watch?v=pfYeHHtj7so.